FURNITURE CITY FEASTS

R E S T O R E D

A COLLECTION OF RECIPES

FROM THE

JUNIOR LEAGUE

OF HIGH POINT

The Mary Strickland Froelich Junior League of High Point, Inc., Headquarters
—THE BRILES HOUSE

*The cover photograph, the architectural insets, and Miss Briles'
Tea Party were shot at this historic home.*

FURNITURE CITY FEASTS
RESTORED

A COLLECTION OF RECIPES FROM THE
JUNIOR LEAGUE OF HIGH POINT

Furniture City Feasts, Restored

Published by the Junior League of High Point, Inc.

Copyright © 2006 by Junior League of High Point, Inc.
707 Westchester Drive, Suite 103
High Point, North Carolina 27262
336-889-5479

Photography © Michael B. Hussey, Jr.

Library of Congress Catalog Number: 2005932630
ISBN: 0-9771791-0-9

Edited, Designed, and Manufactured by Favorite Recipes® Press
An imprint of

FRP

P.O. Box 305142
Nashville, Tennessee 37230
800-358-0560

Art Director: Steve Newman
Book Design: Brad Whitfield and Susan Breining
Project Editor: Tanis Westbrook

Printed in China
First Printing: 2006   10,000 copies

Denotes favorites from *Furniture City Feasts*

Denotes recipes from our past presidents

Denotes recipes in Miss Briles' Tea Party

Denotes recipes in the North Carolina Barbecue Picnic

PREFACE

The Junior League of High Point (JLHP) is an organization of women committed to promoting voluntarism, developing the potential of women, and improving the community through the effective action and leadership of trained volunteers.

In 1928, twenty-four ambitious volunteers joined together to entertain children who were patients at the County Tuberculosis Sanatorium. These dedicated ladies formed the Junior Service League of High Point, which in 1952 became a member of the Association of Junior Leagues International.

For more than seventy-five years, JLHP volunteers have shared their time and talents with the City of High Point. Throughout the League's history, we have started community projects, joined in coalitions with other groups to meet perceived needs, and placed our members in the programs of agencies working to improve the quality of life within our community. Listed below are some of the projects and organizations that the JLHP has supported over the years with volunteer hours and money raised through fund-raisers.

Carousel Theatre

Center School for Exceptional Children

CHILDWATCH

Community Clinic of High Point

Developmental Day Care

Done-in-a-Day Projects

Family Services Bureau

High Point Area Arts Council

High Point Historical Museum

Kids on the Block

Mental Health Association

North Carolina Shakespeare Festival

Piedmont Environmental Center

Roy B. Culler, Jr., Senior Center

Teacher Mini-Grants

Theatre Art Gallery

YWCA

All proceeds from the sale of this book will benefit the community projects of the Junior League of High Point, Inc.

ACKNOWLEDGMENTS

Photography: Michael B. Hussey, Jr.
Art Direction: Evie Cottam, Allison Russell
Line Art: Laurie Tester

Historical information courtesy of the High Point Historical Museum

Past presidents' recipes were included to honor those women who were instrumental in the development and success of the Junior League of High Point, Inc. Their leadership and time commitment to this volunteer organization are greatly appreciated.

COOKBOOK STEERING COMMITTEE

Caryl Adams
Susie Bland
Dorotea Evans
Judy Hustrulid

COOKBOOK COMMITTEE 2005-2006

Cindy Jarrell, *Chair*
Debbie Smothers, *Assistant Chair*

Lynn Bass
MacLean Clinard
Lee Ann Magnusson
Avery Merritt

Catherine Niebauer
Elizabeth Sheffield
Laurie Tester
Nicole Wilson

Chris Amos, *Sustainer Advisor*

INTRODUCTION

Southern hospitality and food are as synonymous with each other as fresh-from-the-oven cookies and a tall glass of cold milk. Southern cooks have long shared their favorite recipes with loved ones during holiday gatherings, as a welcoming gift to a new neighbor who just moved in next door, and as an expression of sympathy for the family of a close friend. Furniture City Feasts, published in 1971, was the first cookbook published by the Junior League of High Point (JLHP). The book was filled with many delectable recipes, which have stood the test of time. Furniture City Feasts, Restored is our newest endeavor to remember and honor the past while forging ahead to the future.

The Briles House, built in 1907 by Mr. and Mrs. Lee A. Briles, was a showcase home on North Main Street that provided an elegant backdrop for many civic and social events of yesteryear. As time passed, the Briles' daughter, Ruth, became the caretaker of the stately Victorian home. She epitomized Southern grace by often inviting friends into her spacious parlor for an afternoon gathering for tea and cookies. Miss Briles continued to live in the home until her death in 2001.

Dedicated to preserving a piece of history, the JLHP purchased the Briles House in 2002, with the help of generous donations from the community. The home will be used as headquarters for the JLHP, as well as a place to host events for the High Point community. In recognition of her contributions to the League on a local and national level, the JLHP chose to memorialize Mazie Froelich by naming the facility "The Mary Strickland Froelich Junior League of High Point, Inc., Headquarters— The Briles House." Mazie served as president of the JLHP in 1969 and later served as a director in the Association of Junior Leagues International.

The philanthropic spirit of Mazie Froelich and the Briles family will continue through the restoration of this historic gem for the High Point community. The exquisite craftsmanship and aesthetic details will shine as the home takes on its new life as a community gathering place. Your purchase of Furniture City Feasts, Restored will help the JLHP to return this gracious Southern home to its original splendor of almost a century ago.

TABLE OF CONTENTS

AWAKENINGS
BREADS BREAKFASTS & BRUNCHES

BEGINNINGS
APPETIZERS BEVERAGES SOUPS & SALADS

CENTERPIECES
MEAT POULTRY SEAFOOD & PASTA

TABLE OF CONTENTS

COMPLEMENTS
VEGETABLES & SIDE DISHES

FINISHES
DESSERTS

FROM OUR LOCAL CHEFS

AWAKENINGS

BREADS
BREAKFASTS
&
BRUNCHES

Stuffed French Toast *page 22*

Poppy Seed Bread

BREAD

3   cups all-purpose flour

2 1/2 cups sugar

1 1/2 teaspoons salt

1 1/2 teaspoon baking powder

3   eggs

1 1/2 cups milk

1   cup plus 2 tablespoons vegetable oil

2   tablespoons poppy seeds

1 1/2 teaspoons butter flavoring

1 1/2 teaspoons vanilla extract

1 1/2 teaspoons almond extract

ORANGE GLAZE

3/4 cup sugar

1/4 cup orange juice

1/2 teaspoon vanilla extract

1/2 teaspoon almond extract

1/2 teaspoon vegetable oil

For the bread, preheat the oven to 350 degrees. Combine the flour, sugar, salt and baking powder in a bowl. Combine the eggs, milk, oil, poppy seeds, butter flavoring, vanilla and almond extract in a large mixing bowl and beat until blended. Add the flour mixture and beat for 2 minutes. Pour into 2 greased and floured loaf pans. Bake for 1 hour. Let cool for 10 minutes.

For the glaze, combine the sugar, orange juice, vanilla, almond extract and oil in a small saucepan over medium heat and cook until the sugar melts, stirring frequently. Poke holes in the warm bread and pour the glaze over the top. Remove the bread from the pans when cool.

Makes 2 loaves

BLUEBERRY MUFFINS

1	cup quick-cooking oats
1	cup buttermilk
1	tablespoon vanilla extract
1	egg
3/4	cup packed light brown sugar
1/4	cup (1/2 stick) butter, softened
1	cup unbleached all-purpose flour
1	tablespoon baking powder
1	teaspoon salt
1	teaspoon cinnamon
1/2	teaspoon baking soda
1/2	teaspoon freshly grated nutmeg
1/4	cup chopped walnuts
1 1/3	cups blueberries

Preheat the oven to 400 degrees. Combine the oats, buttermilk and vanilla in a bowl and mix well. Combine the egg and brown sugar in a large mixing bowl and beat until blended. Add the butter and beat until light and fluffy. Add the oat mixture and mix well. Add the flour, baking powder, salt, cinnamon, baking soda and nutmeg and stir until all the dry ingredients are incorporated. Do not overmix. Fold in the walnuts and blueberries. Fill 18 large buttered muffin cups 1/2 full. Bake on the center rack of the oven for 15 to 20 minutes or until golden brown. Remove to a wire rack to cool.

Serves 18

High Point takes its name from its location on the old North Carolina Railroad. The highest point on the railroad was said to be at its intersection with the Fayetteville and Western Plank Road, where High Point's center developed.

CHEESE KRISPIES

1   stick ($^1/2$ cup) butter
1   cup all-purpose flour
1$^1/2$ cups crisp rice cereal
1   cup (4 ounces) shredded sharp
      Cheddar cheese
      Dash of red pepper flakes

Preheat the oven to 350 degrees. Cream the butter in a mixing bowl. Add the flour gradually, stirring constantly. Add the cereal, cheese and red pepper flakes and mix well. The dough will be stiff. Drop by teaspoonfuls onto a baking sheet. Bake for 10 to 12 minutes.

Serves 12 to 15

BEER BISCUITS

4$^1/2$ cups biscuit baking mix
$^3/4$ cup sugar
1   (12-ounce) can beer

Preheat the oven to 375 degrees. Combine the baking mix, sugar and beer in a bowl and mix well. The batter will be lumpy. Fill greased and floured muffin cups $^2/3$ full. Bake for 20 to 30 minutes or until the tops are puffed and light brown.

Makes about 24 biscuits

CHEESE BISCUITS

1   cup skim milk or buttermilk
1   teaspoon Tabasco sauce
3   cups biscuit baking mix
1   cup (4 ounces) finely shredded
      Cheddar cheese

Preheat the oven to 425 degrees. Combine the milk with the Tabasco sauce in a bowl and mix well. Combine the baking mix and cheese in a large bowl. Add the milk mixture and stir just until the dough is moist. Pat the dough out on a floured surface. Cut with a biscuit cutter. Arrange on a lightly greased baking sheet. Bake for 8 to 10 minutes or until puffy and light brown.

Makes 33 to 35 biscuits

Tip: You may freeze before baking, if desired. Arrange the dough rounds on a baking sheet and freeze. Place the frozen dough rounds in a freezer-safe sealable bag. Let them thaw for 15 to 30 minutes before baking.

Refrigerator Rolls

2	envelopes dry yeast
1	cup warm water
1	cup shortening
1	cup sugar
1	cup boiling water
2	eggs
6	cups all-purpose flour
1	tablespoon salt
	Butter or margarine, melted

Sprinkle the yeast over the warm water in a bowl. Cream the shortening and sugar in a large mixing bowl until light and fluffy. Add the boiling water and mix well. Beat the eggs in a small bowl. Fold into the shortening mixture. Add the yeast mixture. Sift in the flour and salt and mix well. Chill, covered, until ready to prepare. The dough will keep for up to 1 week in the refrigerator. Two to 3 hours before ready to bake, roll the dough to 1/2-inch thickness on a floured surface. Cut with a biscuit cutter. Place a small amount of butter on each round and fold over, pinching the edges to seal. Arrange on a lightly greased baking sheet and brush with melted butter or margarine. Let rise for 2 to 3 hours. Preheat the oven to 400 degrees. Bake the rolls for 10 to 15 minutes or until light brown on top.

Makes about 36 rolls

The YWCA's Famous Rolls

1	envelope dry yeast, or 1 cake compressed yeast
3/4	cup milk, scalded and cooled
3/4	cup lukewarm water
1/4	cup melted shortening
6	tablespoons sugar
1 3/4	teaspoons salt
5	to 5 1/4 cups all-purpose flour
	Butter or margarine, melted

Soften the yeast in the milk in a large bowl. Add the water, shortening, sugar and salt and mix well. Add the flour a small amount at a time, beating well after each addition. Turn onto a lightly floured work surface and knead until smooth. Let rise, covered with a warm damp cloth, until doubled in bulk. Roll to 1/3-inch thickness. Cut into 2-inch rounds. Crease the middle of each round with the dull edge of a knife. Brush half of each round with butter. Fold over, pressing the edges to seal. Arrange on a well-greased baking sheet. Let rise, covered, until tripled in bulk. Preheat the oven to 450 degrees. Bake for 15 to 18 minutes or until light brown on top.

Makes about 24 rolls

Zola's Rolls

1   cup milk, scalded
1/2 cup sugar
1   tablespoon salt
3   envelopes dry yeast
1   cup lukewarm water
2   eggs
7   cups all-purpose flour
1/2 cup vegetable oil

Mix the milk, sugar and salt in a bowl and let cool. Dissolve the yeast in the water in a bowl and let stand until foamy and doubled in volume. Beat the eggs in a large bowl. Add the milk mixture and yeast mixture and mix well. Add 4 cups of the flour, the oil and the remaining 3 cups flour, mixing well after each addition and adding additional flour if the dough is sticky. Let rise, covered, for 1 1/2 hours. Roll out on a lightly floured surface. Shape into rolls and arrange on a greased baking sheet. Let rise until doubled in bulk. Preheat the oven to 400 degrees. Bake for 15 minutes.

Makes about 40 rolls

Zola's Corn Bread

1   cup self-rising cornmeal
3   eggs
1/2 cup vegetable oil
1   (8-ounce) can cream-style corn
1/2 cup sour cream
1   tablespoon sugar

Preheat the oven to 425 degrees. Mix the cornmeal, eggs, oil, corn, sour cream and sugar in a bowl. Spoon into a square baking dish. Bake for 25 minutes.

Serves 8

MEXICAN CORN BREAD

1   cup yellow or white cornmeal
1   (8-ounce) can cream-style corn
3   eggs, beaten
3/4 cup milk
1/2 cup canola oil or vegetable oil
1   teaspoon salt
1   teaspoon baking soda
3   (4-ounce) cans chopped green
     chiles, drained
1   cup (4 ounces) shredded sharp
     Cheddar cheese

Preheat the oven to 375 degrees. Combine the cornmeal, corn, eggs, milk, oil, salt, baking soda, green chiles and cheese in a bowl and mix well. Pour into a square baking dish. Bake for 1 hour.

Serves 8

Nancy Lyles, President 1957–1958

PIZZA DOUGH

2   envelopes dry yeast
1/2 cup very warm water
3   cups bread flour
1   teaspoon salt
1/2 cup very warm water
1   tablespoon olive oil

Dissolve the yeast in 1/2 cup water in a small bowl. Let stand for 5 minutes or until foamy. Combine the remaining ingredients in a food processor fitted with a knife blade and process until the mixture resembles coarse crumbs. Add the yeast mixture gradually, processing constantly until the dough forms a loose ball. The dough will be sticky. Grease your hands and shape the dough into a ball. Place the dough in a greased bowl, turning to coat the surface. Let rise, covered, in a warm place for 1 hour or until doubled in bulk. Punch the dough down. Divide the dough into halves and place each half on a greased pizza pan. Let rise, covered, in a warm place for 1 hour. Preheat the oven to 450 degrees. Pat the dough out to the desired thickness. Top with your favorite pizza sauce, toppings and cheese. Bake on the lowest rack in the oven until the crust is light brown and the cheese is melted.

Makes 2 pizza crusts

Lee Worden, President 1993–1994

Blue Cheese Bread

1   (12-ounce) loaf crusty French bread
1/2   cup (1 stick) butter, softened
4   ounces blue cheese, crumbled

Preheat the oven to 375 degrees. Cut the bread into 3/4-inch slices, cutting to but not through the bottom. Combine the butter and cheese in a small bowl and mix well. Spread the mixture evenly over both sides of each bread slice. Wrap the bread in aluminum foil and place on a baking sheet. Bake for 7 minutes or until golden brown.

Serves 6 to 8

Tasty Cheesy Garlic Bread

1   loaf sourdough bread or French bread
1 1/2 cups (6 ounces) grated Romano cheese
1   cup mayonnaise
     Juice of 1/2 lemon
2   tablespoons white wine (optional)
3   tablespoons butter, softened
1/2   cup chopped fresh parsley
2   garlic cloves, minced

Preheat the oven to 425 degrees. Cut the bread into halves lengthwise and place on a baking sheet. Combine the cheese, mayonnaise, lemon juice, wine, butter, parsley and garlic in a bowl and mix well. Spread over the cut side of the bread. Bake for 10 minutes or until the cheese is light brown and bubbly and the bread is crisp. Serve hot.

Serves 10 to 12

Cheddar-Baked English Muffins

1 1/2 cups (6 ounces) shredded sharp
    Cheddar cheese
1/2 cup mayonnaise
1 (3-ounce) can black olives, drained
    and chopped
1/2 cup chopped scallions
1 garlic clove, minced, or 1/2 teaspoon
    garlic powder
1/2 teaspoon curry powder
    Pepper to taste
4 English muffins, halved, or 8 miniature
    English muffins, halved

Preheat the oven to 450 degrees. Combine
the cheese, mayonnaise, black olives,
scallions, garlic, curry powder and pepper
in a bowl and mix well. You may prepare
to this point 1 day in advance and chill,
covered, until ready to use. Spread the
mixture over the cut sides of the muffins.
Arrange on a baking sheet. Bake for
10 minutes.

Serves 8

Pull-Apart Breakfast Bread

1 stick (1/2 cup) butter
1/2 cup packed brown sugar
1 (4-ounce) package vanilla
    cook-and-serve pudding mix
1 teaspoon cinnamon
3/4 cup chopped pecans
1/2 cup raisins (optional)
18 frozen Parker House rolls

Combine the butter, brown sugar, pudding
mix and cinnamon in a small saucepan and
heat until the butter is melted, stirring
frequently. Sprinkle the pecans and raisins
over the bottom of a well-buttered tube
pan. Layer the rolls evenly in the prepared
pan. Pour the pudding mixture over the
rolls. Let stand, covered with a towel, for
8 to 10 hours. Preheat a standard oven to
350 degrees or a convection oven to
325 degrees. Place the pan on aluminum
foil in the oven. Bake for 25 minutes in
a standard oven or for 20 minutes in a
convection oven. Cool in the pan for
10 minutes. Invert onto a serving plate.

Serves 8 to 10

Honey Bun Coffee Cake

COFFEE CAKE

1	(2-layer) package yellow cake mix
1/2	cup granulated sugar
3/4	cup vegetable oil
4	eggs
1	cup sour cream
1	cup packed brown sugar
1	tablespoon cinnamon

GLAZE (optional)

1/2	(16-ounce) package confectioners' sugar
1/4	cup (1/2 stick) butter, melted
	Warm water

For the coffee cake, preheat the oven to 300 degrees. Combine the cake mix, granulated sugar, oil and eggs in a mixing bowl and beat until blended. Add the sour cream and mix well. Pour into a lightly greased and floured 11×13-inch baking pan. Combine the brown sugar and cinnamon in a small bowl and mix well. Sprinkle over the batter and swirl into the batter with a knife. Bake for 45 to 60 minutes or until the coffee cake tests done. Let stand until cool.

For the glaze, combine the confectioners' sugar and butter in a small bowl. Add enough water to thin the glaze to the desired consistency. Drizzle over the cooled coffee cake.

Serves 16 to 18

Sour Cream Coffee Cakes to Share

2   cups (4 sticks) butter, softened
4   cups sugar
4   eggs
2   cups sour cream
1   teaspoon vanilla extract
2   teaspoons baking powder
1   teaspoon salt
4   cups all-purpose flour, sifted
8   teaspoons sugar
2   teaspoons cinnamon
2   cups chopped pecans

Preheat the oven to 350 degrees. Cream the butter and 4 cups sugar in a mixing bowl until light and fluffy. Add the eggs 1 at a time, beating well after each addition. Add the sour cream, vanilla, baking powder and salt and mix well. Fold in the flour and mix well. Divide half the batter evenly among 3 round baking pans. Combine 8 teaspoons sugar and the cinnamon in a small bowl. Sprinkle half the pecans evenly over the batter. Sprinkle with half the cinnamon mixture. Pour the remaining batter over the layers. Top with the remaining pecans and cinnamon mixture. Bake for 45 to 50 minutes or until the coffee cakes test done.

Makes 3 coffee cakes

Tip: *For easy gift-giving, use disposable aluminum pans. These cakes freeze well. Eat 1 cake now, and freeze the remaining 2 for later use.*

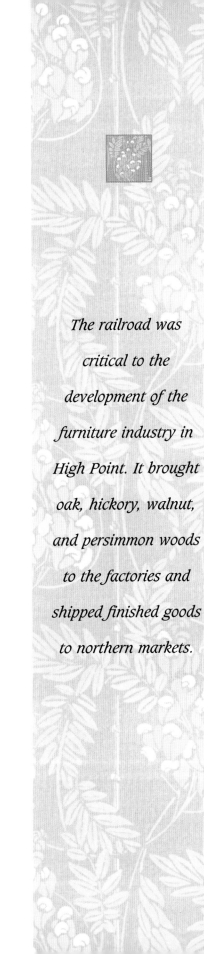

The railroad was critical to the development of the furniture industry in High Point. It brought oak, hickory, walnut, and persimmon woods to the factories and shipped finished goods to northern markets.

OVERNIGHT FRENCH TOAST

3/4 cup (1 1/2 sticks) butter
1 cup packed brown sugar
2 tablespoons corn syrup
12 slices bread
1 (16-ounce) carton pasteurized
egg substitute
1 cup milk
1 teaspoon vanilla extract

Combine the butter, brown sugar and corn syrup in a skillet and simmer until slightly thickened, stirring frequently. Pour into a 9×13-inch baking dish. Arrange the bread in 2 layers over the syrup. Combine the egg substitute, milk and vanilla in a bowl and beat until blended. Pour over the bread. Chill, covered with aluminum foil, for 8 to 10 hours. Preheat the oven to 350 degrees. Bake, covered, for 35 minutes. Remove the aluminum foil and bake for 10 minutes longer.

Serves 6 to 10

STUFFED FRENCH TOAST

1 loaf French bread, cut into 16 slices
11 ounces cream cheese, sliced
12 eggs
2 cups milk
1/3 cup maple syrup
Dash of cinnamon

Arrange 8 bread slices in a single layer in a greased 9×13-inch baking dish. Layer the cream cheese over the bread. Layer the remaining bread on top. Combine the eggs, milk, maple syrup and cinnamon in a large bowl and whisk until blended. Pour over the bread. Chill, covered, for 8 hours or longer. Let stand at room temperature for 30 minutes. Preheat the oven to 350 degrees. Bake, uncovered, for 20 minutes. Cover with aluminum foil and bake for 25 minutes longer. Serve with hot maple syrup.

Makes 8 servings

Tip: *This is best made with real cream cheese. Do not substitute low-fat or fat-free cream cheese.*

The photograph for this recipe appears on page 10.

Buttermilk Pancakes

1²/3 cups all-purpose flour
1/3 cup cornmeal
1/4 cup sugar
2 teaspoons baking soda
1 teaspoon salt
2 eggs
2 cups buttermilk
2 tablespoons butter, melted

Preheat a lightly greased griddle or heavy skillet over medium heat. Sift together the flour, cornmeal, sugar, baking soda and salt into a large bowl. Beat the eggs in a bowl. Add the buttermilk and butter and mix until blended. Pour the buttermilk mixture into the flour mixture and stir just until moistened. There will be lumps in the batter. Pour 1/4 cup of the batter for standard-size pancakes or 1 tablespoon batter for dollar-size pancakes onto the heated griddle. Cook until the top just begins to bubble and the bottom is golden brown. Turn the pancakes and cook for 1 minute or until light brown.

Makes about 18 standard-size pancakes or about 75 dollar-size pancakes

Corn Patties

4 small ears tender white corn
1 cup all-purpose flour
1 tablespoon cornmeal
1 teaspoon baking powder
1/2 teaspoon salt
1¹/2 cups buttermilk
1 egg, beaten
1/2 teaspoon baking soda
1 tablespoon corn oil

Preheat a griddle over medium heat. Cut the corn kernels from the cobs. Sift together the flour, cornmeal, baking powder and salt into a bowl. Add the buttermilk, egg and baking soda and stir until blended and just beginning to bubble. Add the corn oil and corn kernels and mix well. Pour small amounts of the batter onto the griddle. Cook until the tops begin to bubble. Turn and cook until golden brown. Serve hot with syrup.

Serves 6

Never-Fail Waffles

1 1/3 cups all-purpose flour, sifted
1 heaping tablespoon baking powder
1/2 teaspoon salt
1 egg, beaten
6 tablespoons vegetable oil
1 1/2 cups milk
1 teaspoon sugar

Preheat a waffle iron. Combine the flour, baking powder and salt in a bowl. Combine the egg and oil in a bowl and beat until blended. Add the milk and mix well. Add the flour mixture and sugar and mix until blended. Pour about 1/2 cup batter onto the waffle iron. Bake using the manufacturer's directions.

Makes about 6 waffles

Nan Kester, President 1981–1982

Cheese Soufflé

8 slices white bread, cut into pieces
2 cups (8 ounces) sharp Cheddar cheese, shredded
3 or 4 eggs, beaten
2 cups milk
1 teaspoon dry mustard
1/2 teaspoon salt
Pepper to taste

Preheat the oven to 350 degrees. Arrange the bread in a rectangular baking dish. Top with the cheese. Combine the eggs, milk, dry mustard, salt and pepper in a bowl and beat until blended. Pour over the cheese layer. Bake for 1 hour.

Serves 6 to 8

Sausage and Brie Soufflé

6 slices white bread
1 pound bulk hot pork sausage, browned and drained
12 ounces Brie cheese, rind removed and cheese cubed
1 cup (4 ounces) freshly grated Parmesan cheese
5 eggs
3 cups whipping cream, heavy cream or half-and-half
2 cups milk
1 1/2 tablespoons chopped fresh sage
1 teaspoon salt
2 eggs

Trim the crusts from the bread and arrange the crusts in a lightly greased 9×13-inch baking dish. Layer the bread slices, sausage, Brie cheese and Parmesan cheese in the prepared dish. Whisk 5 eggs and 2 cups of the cream in a bowl. Add the milk, sage and salt and mix well. Pour over the layers. Chill, covered, for 8 hours or longer. Preheat the oven to 350 degrees. Combine 2 eggs and the remaining cream in a bowl and whisk until blended. Pour over the layers. Bake for 1 hour or until the center is set.

Serves 8 to 10

Donna Blakely, President 2005–2006

Sausage Strata

1 1/2 pounds bulk pork sausage
1 teaspoon prepared mustard
6 slices bread, crusts trimmed
1 cup (4 ounces) shredded Swiss cheese
4 eggs, lightly beaten
1 1/2 cups milk
3/4 cup light cream
1 teaspoon Worcestershire sauce
1/2 teaspoon salt
Dash of pepper
Dash of nutmeg

Preheat the oven to 350 degrees. Brown the sausage in a skillet, stirring until crumbly; drain. Stir in the mustard. Arrange the bread in a large greased baking dish. Top with the sausage. Sprinkle with the cheese. Combine the eggs, milk, cream, Worcestershire sauce, salt, pepper and nutmeg in a bowl and beat until blended. Pour over the cheese layer. Bake for 30 minutes or until the center is set.

Serves 4 to 6

Helen Covington, President 1958–1959

Tip: You may make this in advance and keep chilled in the refrigerator until ready to bake. For a dinner entrée, add chopped onions to the sausage when browning.

CRAN-APPLE CRUMBLE

3   cups sliced apples
2   cups fresh cranberries
1 1/2 cups granulated sugar
1/2 cup water
1/2 cup (1 stick) butter
1/2 cup packed brown sugar
1 1/2 cups rolled oats
1/3 cup all-purpose flour
1/2 cup chopped pecans

Preheat the oven to 350 degrees. Layer the apples, cranberries and granulated sugar in a greased 1 1/2- or 2-quart baking dish. Pour the water over the fruit. Heat the butter and brown sugar in a saucepan until the butter is melted, stirring frequently. Add the oats, flour and pecans and mix well. Pour over the fruit. Bake for 1 hour. Let stand for 10 to 15 minutes before serving.

Serves 6 to 8

Peggy Amos, President 1963–1964

BROCCOLI AND CHEESE BREAKFAST BAKE

4   eggs, or an equivalent amount of pasteurized egg substitute
1/3 cup whole milk or skim milk
1   tablespoon mayonnaise
1   tablespoon sour cream
1   (8-ounce) package yellow corn muffin mix
1   tablespoon sugar
1   (10-ounce) package frozen chopped broccoli, cooked and drained
1/2 cup chopped onion (optional)
2   cups (8 ounces) shredded Cheddar cheese

Preheat the oven to 425 degrees. Combine the eggs, milk, mayonnaise and sour cream in a large bowl and beat until blended. Stir in the corn muffin mix and sugar. Add the broccoli, onion and cheese and mix well. Spoon into a 9-inch springform pan, round baking pan or cast-iron skillet lightly coated with cooking spray. Bake for 25 to 35 minutes or until the edge is crispy and brown.

Makes 8 to 10 servings

CHEESY HASH BROWNS

1	(32-ounce) package frozen hash brown potatoes, thawed
1/2	cup (1 stick) butter or margarine, melted
1/2	cup chopped onion
1	(10-ounce) can cream of chicken soup
1	cup sour cream
1	cup (4 ounces) shredded Cheddar cheese
1	cup crushed cornflakes
1/4	cup (1/2 stick) butter or margarine, melted
	Parsley sprigs

Preheat the oven to 350 degrees. Combine the potatoes, 1/2 cup butter, the onion, soup, sour cream and cheese in a large bowl and mix well. Spoon into a greased 2 1/2-quart baking dish. Combine the cornflakes and 1/4 cup butter in a bowl and mix well. Sprinkle over the potato mixture. Bake for 50 minutes. Garnish with parsley.

Serves 8 to 10

SPECK AND DICKEN

1	pound ground beef
1	pound bulk pork sausage
4	eggs
4	cups buttermilk
1	cup dark corn syrup
5 1/2	cups all-purpose flour
2	cups packed brown sugar
1/2	cup granulated sugar
2	teaspoons baking soda
2	teaspoons salt

Combine the ground beef and sausage in a bowl and mix well. Shape into very thin patties no larger than 2 inches in diameter. Arrange on waxed paper and chill in the refrigerator until ready to use.

Preheat a lightly greased griddle. Combine the eggs, buttermilk, corn syrup, flour, brown sugar, granulated sugar, baking soda and salt in a large bowl and mix well. Arrange the meat patties 6 inches apart on the griddle. Cook until brown on 1 side. Turn the patties over and pour batter over each. Do not allow more than 1 1/2 inches of batter to run beyond the edge of the patties. Cook until the batter begins to bubble. Turn and cook until the pancakes are golden brown.

Serves about 8

BEGINNINGS

APPETIZERS
BEVERAGES
SOUPS
&
SALADS

Pesto Pinwheels

1   (4- or 8-count) package refrigerator
       crescent rolls
       Prepared pesto
       Grated Parmesan cheese
       Diced red bell pepper, or pine nuts
       (optional)

Preheat the oven to 375 degrees. Unroll
the crescent roll dough on a cutting board
and separate into rectangles, pressing the
perforations together. Spread with pesto and
sprinkle with Parmesan cheese. Roll up each
rectangle as for a jelly roll and cut into
1/2-inch slices. Place the pinwheels cut side
down on a baking sheet. Garnish the center
with bell pepper or pine nuts, if desired.
Bake for 10 minutes or until golden brown.

Makes 24 or 48 pinwheels

Party Cucumber Sandwiches

8   ounces cream cheese, softened
2   tablespoons mayonnaise
1/4   to 1/2 teaspoon seasoned salt
       Chopped chives
       Sandwich bread slices, cut with
       cookie cutters into rounds or other
       desired shapes
       Thinly sliced cucumbers
       Freshly ground pepper

Combine the cream cheese, mayonnaise,
seasoned salt and chives in a mixing bowl
and beat until light and fluffy. Chill for
1 hour or longer. Spread the mixture on
the bread and top each with a cucumber
slice. Sprinkle with the pepper.

Makes 18 to 24 appetizers

Sausage and Cheese Party Puffs

1   pound bulk pork country sausage
1   pound (4 cups) shredded sharp
       Cheddar cheese
3   cups biscuit baking mix
       Chopped onion and celery (optional)
       Dash of garlic powder (optional)
       Red pepper flakes (optional)

Preheat the oven to 350 degrees. Combine the sausage, cheese, baking mix, onion, celery, garlic powder and red pepper flakes in a large bowl and mix well using your hands. Shape into bite-size balls. Place on a baking sheet. Bake for 10 to 12 minutes or until golden brown. Serve hot with wooden picks.

Makes 10 to 12 dozen appetizers

Tip: These puffs can be made ahead and frozen.

Make-Ahead Ham and Cheese Rolls

1   (48-count) package small dinner rolls
1/4   cup (1/2 stick) butter or margarine
1   tablespoon (or more) poppy seeds
1   tablespoon prepared mustard
1   (6-ounce) package sliced Swiss cheese
       (12 slices), quartered
6   to 8 ounces thinly sliced cooked
       ham, quartered

Remove the rolls from the package, reserving the foil pan. Separate the rolls using a sharp knife. Slice each roll into halves horizontally, keeping the 2 halves together. Combine the butter, poppy seeds and mustard in a small saucepan or microwave-safe bowl and heat until the butter is melted. Brush the butter mixture on the cut side of the rolls. Layer the cheese and ham slices on the bottom half of each roll. Cover with the top half. Place the filled rolls in the reserved foil pan and wrap tightly with heavy-duty foil. Freeze for up to 1 month. Preheat the oven to 350 degrees. Bake the rolls in the foil-wrapped pan for 5 to 10 minutes or until the cheese is melted.

Serves 24

Artichoke Squares

2   (6-ounce) jars marinated
    artichoke hearts
1   onion, chopped
1   garlic clove, minced
2   eggs
1/4   cup bread crumbs
    Dash of Tabasco sauce
1/2   teaspoon oregano
    Salt and pepper
1   cup (4 ounces) shredded
    Cheddar cheese

Preheat the oven to 325 degrees. Drain the marinade from 1 jar of the artichokes into a skillet. Add the onion and garlic and sauté until tender. Drain the remaining jar of artichokes, discarding the marinade. Chop all of the artichokes. Beat the eggs in a large bowl. Add the bread crumbs, Tabasco sauce, oregano, salt and pepper and mix well. Stir in the onion mixture, artichokes and cheese. Pour into a lightly greased 9×13-inch baking dish. Bake for 30 minutes. Cool in the dish for 5 minutes. Cut into squares and serve hot.

Makes about 25 squares

Mahogany Mushrooms

2   cups (4 sticks) unsalted butter
4   cups burgundy
1 1/2   tablespoons Worcestershire sauce
1   teaspoon dill seeds
1   teaspoon garlic powder
1   teaspoon pepper
1/2   teaspoon salt, or to taste
4   beef bouillon cubes
4   chicken bouillon cubes
2   cups boiling water
4   pounds small fresh mushrooms

Melt the butter in a large kettle or Dutch oven. Add the wine, Worcestershire sauce, dill seeds, garlic powder, pepper and salt. Dissolve the beef and chicken bouillon cubes in the boiling water and add to the pan. Stir in the mushrooms. Bring to a boil over medium heat. Reduce the heat and simmer, covered, for 5 to 6 hours or until the liquid is reduced, stirring occasionally. Taste and adjust the seasonings. Serve hot in a chafing dish with wooden picks.

Makes 12 to 16 servings

Tip: This dish can be made several days ahead and frozen.

Cheese Ball with Chutney

2   cups (8 ounces) Cheddar
    cheese, shredded
4   ounces cream cheese, softened
2   tablespoons dry sherry
1   garlic clove, minced
1   (15-ounce) jar mango chutney
5   slices bacon, crisp-cooked
    and crumbled
3   green onions, chopped

Combine the Cheddar cheese, cream cheese, sherry and garlic in a bowl and beat well. Shape into a ball and place on a serving dish. Pour the chutney over the cheese ball and sprinkle with the bacon and green onions. Serve with assorted crackers.

Makes 16 appetizer servings

Cheddar and Pecan Cheese Balls

32 ounces cream cheese, softened
4   cups (16 ounces) shredded extra-sharp
    Cheddar cheese
1/2 cup chopped pecans
1/2 teaspoon salt
1/4 teaspoon garlic powder
1   pinch of baking soda
1/4 cup evaporated milk
1/2 cup chopped pecans

Beat the cream cheese in a large mixing bowl until light and fluffy. Stir in the Cheddar cheese and 1/2 cup pecans. Add the salt, garlic powder, baking soda and evaporated milk and mix well. Shape into 4 balls and roll in 1/2 cup pecans. Wrap in plastic wrap and chill until firm. Serve with assorted crackers.

Makes 48 to 60 appetizer servings

Baked Gouda in Pastry

1   (8-ounce) Gouda cheese round
     Dijon mustard
1   (8-count) package refrigerator
     crescent rolls
1   egg yolk, beaten

Preheat the oven to 375 degrees. Remove the wax coating from the cheese and spread the cheese round with Dijon mustard. Unroll the crescent roll dough on a cutting board and separate into 2 large rectangles, pressing the perforations together. Place the cheese round on 1 of the dough rectangles and cover with the second rectangle. Pinch the edges of the dough together to seal, trimming as needed. Cut decorative shapes from the remaining dough to garnish the top, if desired. Brush the dough with the egg yolk and place on a baking sheet. Bake for 10 to 15 minutes or until browned. Cut into wedges. Serve with apple or pear slices or crackers.

Makes 16 to 24 appetizer servings

Tomato-Cheddar Spread

1   (10-ounce) can diced tomatoes with
     green chiles, drained
1   cup mayonnaise
1   teaspoon Worcestershire sauce
1/2 teaspoon salt
2   (8-ounce) blocks sharp Cheddar
     cheese, shredded (pre-shredded cheese
     not recommended)
1   (4-ounce) jar chopped
     pimentos, drained

Stir together the tomatoes with green chiles, mayonnaise, Worcestershire sauce and salt in a large bowl. Add the cheese and pimentos and mix well. Spoon into a serving dish and serve with crackers.

Makes about 6 cups

Julie Walters, President 1998–1999

Tip: This can also be used as a sandwich spread.

Pâté Maison Three Musketeers

1   pound larding pork, diced (ask your butcher)
1   onion, finely chopped
4   shallots, chopped
2   small garlic cloves, finely chopped
    Pinch of thyme
1   bay leaf
3   pounds chicken livers
3/4 cup dry white wine
1   pound (4 sticks) butter, melted
1/2 cup each dry sherry and Cognac
    Salt and pepper to taste

Melt the larding pork in a large saucepan over low heat and add the onion, shallots, garlic, thyme and bay leaf. Add the chicken livers and wine and cook for about 10 minutes, stirring occasionally. Remove the bay leaf. Remove the mixture from the pan and purée in batches in a blender until smooth. Pour the liver purée into a bowl and place the bowl in a large container filled with cracked ice to chill the mixture. Return the liver mixture to the blender and add the melted butter gradually, blending constantly until smooth. Add the sherry, Cognac, salt and pepper and blend until light and fluffy. Pour the mixture into a tureen or other serving dish and chill. Serve with thin whole wheat crackers.

Makes about 8 cups

Meredith Slane, President 1942–1944

Tip: This liver pâté can also be used to stuff tomatoes for an elegant luncheon dish.

The first furniture factory in town, High Point Furniture Company, opened in 1889 with a workforce of twenty-five to fifty men. The first piece they made was a desk for the office of the new company.

Hot Artichoke Dip

2   (15-ounce) cans artichoke
     hearts, drained
1   cup mayonnaise
1   cup (4 ounces) grated
     Parmesan cheese
1   tablespoon grated onion
     Juice of 1 lemon

Preheat the oven to 325 degrees. Combine
the artichokes, mayonnaise, cheese, onion
and lemon juice in a bowl and mix well.
Pour into a small shallow baking dish. Bake
for 15 to 20 minutes or until the top is
browned. Serve hot with melba toast.

Makes about 3 1/2 cups

Lane Fulton, President 1970–1971

Summer BLT Dip

2   pounds sliced bacon, crisp-cooked
     and crumbled
1   cup mayonnaise
1   cup sour cream
     Lettuce leaves
4   or 5 firm ripe tomatoes, seeded
     and diced

Combine the bacon, mayonnaise and sour
cream in a large bowl. Chill, covered, for
several hours or overnight. Line a serving
bowl with lettuce and fill with the bacon
mixture. Top with the tomatoes. Serve
with crackers.

Makes about 5 cups

Nancy Anderson, President 1983–1984

Mexican Chili Dip

8   ounces cream cheese, softened
1   (15-ounce) can chili with beans
1   (4-ounce) can diced green chiles
2   cups (8 ounces) Monterey Jack
     cheese, shredded
6   green onions, chopped
1   (4-ounce) can sliced black olives
8   to 10 pimento-stuffed green
     olives, sliced

Preheat the oven to 350 degrees. Spread the cream cheese in a small shallow baking dish. Layer evenly with the chili, green chiles, Monterey Jack cheese, green onions, black olives and green olives. Bake for 20 minutes or until hot and bubbly. Serve with corn chips.

Makes about 6 cups

Tip: *This dip can also be heated in the microwave on High for 3 to 5 minutes.*

Hot Crab Meat Dip

2   teaspoons lemon juice
1   (6-ounce) can crab meat, drained
     and flaked
4   ounces cream cheese, softened
1   cup sour cream
1/4 cup mayonnaise
1   teaspoon garlic salt
1   teaspoon minced onion
1/2 teaspoon minced chives
1/4 teaspoon Worcestershire sauce
1/8 teaspoon salt
2   or 3 drops of Tabasco sauce

Sprinkle the lemon juice over the crab meat. Combine the cream cheese, sour cream, mayonnaise, garlic salt, onion, chives, Worcestershire sauce, salt and Tabasco sauce in a saucepan and mix well. Stir in the crab meat. Cook over low heat until hot, stirring occasionally. Pour into a chafing dish and serve warm with crackers or crusty bread slices.

Makes about 2 1/2 cups

Tip: *Fat-free or low-fat cream cheese and sour cream can be used in this recipe.*

Hot Jalapeño Crab Dip

1	pound lump crab meat, shells removed
1	cup (4 ounces) shredded pepper jack cheese
1/2	cup pickled sliced jalapeño chiles, chopped
1/2	cup mayonnaise
1	garlic clove, minced
1	teaspoon Worcestershire sauce
1	teaspoon Texas Pete hot sauce
1/2	teaspoon salt
1/2	cup (2 ounces) freshly grated Parmesan cheese

Preheat the oven to 350 degrees. Combine the crab meat, pepper jack cheese, jalapeños, mayonnaise, garlic, Worcestershire sauce, hot sauce and salt in a large bowl and toss gently to combine. Pour into a shallow baking dish and sprinkle with the Parmesan cheese. Bake for 25 minutes or until golden brown and bubbly. Serve with toasted pita triangles.

Makes about 4 cups

Baked Ham Dip

16	ounces cream cheese, softened
1	cup sour cream
1	cup chopped cooked ham
1/4	cup minced onion
1/2	teaspoon garlic powder
1	tablespoon butter
1/2	teaspoon Worcestershire sauce
1	cup chopped pecans

Preheat the oven to 350 degrees. Beat the cream cheese in a medium mixing bowl until light and fluffy. Add the sour cream, ham, onion and garlic powder and mix well. Pour into a greased 1-quart baking dish. Melt the butter with the Worcestershire sauce in a small skillet and add the pecans. Sauté until lightly browned. Sprinkle over the ham mixture. Bake for 20 minutes or until hot and bubbly. Serve with crackers or bread cubes.

Makes about 5 cups

Tip: This dip can be made ahead and refrigerated or frozen, unbaked, until ready to serve. Increase the baking time by 5 to 10 minutes.

Olive Dip

8	ounces cream cheese, softened
1/2	cup mayonnaise
1	cup pimento-stuffed green olives, drained and chopped
1	cup finely chopped pecans
2	tablespoons liquid drained from the olives

Beat the cream cheese in a medium mixing bowl until fluffy. Add the mayonnaise, olives, pecans and olive liquid and mix well. Spoon into a serving dish. Serve with thin wheat crackers.

Makes about 3 1/2 cups

Vidalia Onion Dip

2	tablespoons butter
3	large Vidalia onions or other sweet onions, coarsely chopped
2	cups (8 ounces) shredded Swiss cheese
2	cups mayonnaise
1	(8-ounce) can sliced water chestnuts, drained and finely chopped
1/4	cup dry white wine
1	garlic clove, minced
1/2	teaspoon hot red pepper sauce

Preheat the oven to 375 degrees. Melt the butter in a large skillet over medium-high heat and add the onions. Sauté for 10 minutes or until tender. Combine the cheese, mayonnaise, water chestnuts, wine, garlic and hot sauce in a large bowl. Add the onions and mix well. Pour into a lightly greased 2-quart baking dish. Bake for 25 minutes. Let stand for 10 minutes before serving. Serve with tortilla chips or crackers.

Makes about 8 cups

Tip: *For a flavor variation, add lightly sautéed prosciutto before baking.*

Baked Spinach Dip

2　(10-ounce) packages frozen chopped spinach
1　cup boiling water
2　tablespoons butter or margarine
2　tablespoons all-purpose flour
1　(5-ounce) can evaporated milk
2　cups (8 ounces) shredded pepper jack cheese
1　onion, finely chopped
1　teaspoon pepper
3/4　teaspoon celery salt
1/2　teaspoon garlic powder
3　tablespoons Worcestershire sauce

Preheat the oven to 350 degrees. Add the spinach to the boiling water in a saucepan or microwave-safe bowl and heat just until thawed. Drain, reserving 1/2 cup of the liquid. Melt the butter in a medium saucepan. Stir in the flour until smooth. Add the reserved spinach liquid and the evaporated milk and cook until thickened and bubbly, stirring constantly. Add the cheese, onion, pepper, celery salt, garlic powder and Worcestershire sauce and cook over medium-low heat until the cheese is melted, stirring occasionally. Stir in the spinach. Pour into a small baking dish coated with nonstick cooking spray. Bake for 20 minutes. Let stand for 5 to 10 minutes before serving. Serve with warm flour tortillas or tortilla chips.

Makes about 4 cups

Sun-Dried Tomato Dip

1　cup boiling water
1　(3-ounce) package sun-dried tomatoes
1/3　cup finely chopped fresh basil leaves (do not use dried basil)
2　tablespoons balsamic vinegar
2　tablespoons tomato paste
1　tablespoon olive oil
1　garlic clove, minced
1/8　teaspoon salt
1/8　teaspoon pepper
1　(15-ounce) can white beans, rinsed and drained

Pour the boiling water over the sun-dried tomatoes in a bowl and let stand for 15 minutes or until soft. Drain the tomatoes in a strainer, reserving 1/2 cup of the liquid. Put the tomatoes, reserved liquid, basil, vinegar, tomato paste, olive oil, garlic, salt, pepper and beans in a food processor or blender and process until smooth. Pour into a serving bowl and chill for 30 minutes or longer. Serve with pita chips or crackers.

Makes 2 1/2 cups

Beau Monde Dip

2/3   cup mayonnaise
2/3   cup sour cream
1   tablespoon parsley flakes
2   tablespoons dried minced onion
1   teaspoon dill weed
1   teaspoon Beau Monde seasoning

Combine the mayonnaise, sour cream, parsley, onion, dill weed and Beau Monde seasoning in a bowl and mix well. Chill, covered, to allow the flavors to blend. Serve with fresh vegetables, cheese or ham.

Makes 1 1/3 cups

Fruit Dip

8   ounces cream cheese, softened
1   (7-ounce) jar marshmallow creme
2   teaspoons amaretto or
       orange-flavor liqueur
1/4   cup milk

Combine the cream cheese and marshmallow creme in a mixing bowl and beat until fluffy. Add the amaretto and milk, mixing after each addition until smooth. Chill until ready to serve. Serve with assorted fresh fruits.

Makes about 2 cups

Cheddar Cheese Stars

1   cup (2 sticks) butter, softened
1/2   cup (1 stick) margarine, softened
3   cups (12 ounces) sharp Cheddar
       cheese, shredded
1   cup (4 ounces) medium Cheddar
       cheese, shredded
3 1/2 cups all-purpose flour
1   teaspoon salt
1/4   teaspoon cayenne pepper

Preheat the oven to 375 degrees. Combine the butter, margarine and Cheddar cheeses in a large mixing bowl and beat until combined. Add the flour, salt and cayenne pepper and mix well. Shape the dough into a ball and then into 2 logs. Force each log of dough into a cookie press with star design and press onto an ungreased baking sheet. Bake for 10 to 12 minutes or until lightly browned. Bake for 1 to 2 minutes longer for a crispier consistency, watching carefully to avoid overbrowning.

Makes about 48 cheese stars

Dilly Crackers

1/2   cup canola oil or olive oil
1 1/2 teaspoons dill weed
1/4   teaspoon garlic powder
1   envelope ranch salad dressing mix
1   (12- to 14-ounce) package small
      oyster crackers

Preheat the oven to 250 degrees. Whisk
together the canola oil, dill weed, garlic
powder and ranch salad dressing mix in a
large bowl until combined. Add the crackers
and stir until the oil is absorbed. Spread on
a baking sheet or sheet pan and bake for
15 to 20 minutes. Cool on paper towels.
Store in an airtight container.

Serves 20 to 25

Sweet-and-Spicy Pecans

4   cups pecan halves
3   tablespoons coffee-flavor liqueur
1   tablespoon vegetable oil
1/4   cup chili powder
3   tablespoons sugar
1/2   teaspoon salt
1/4   teaspoon cayenne pepper

Preheat the oven to 300 degrees. Combine
the pecans, liqueur and oil in a large bowl
and stir well to coat. Add the chili powder,
sugar, salt and cayenne pepper and toss well
to coat. Spread the pecans in a 10×15-inch
baking pan. Bake for 25 minutes, stirring
frequently. Remove from the oven and
stir with a metal spatula to loosen the
pecans. Let cool before serving. Store in
an airtight container.

Makes about 4 cups

*Tip: These pecans are also delicious as a topping
for tossed green salads, especially in combination
with blue cheese and apples or pears.*

Party Pecans

1	egg white
2	tablespoons cold water
1/2	cup sugar
1/2	teaspoon salt
1/4	teaspoon ground allspice
1/4	teaspoon ground cinnamon
1/4	teaspoon ground cloves
4	cups pecan halves
1/2	cup (1 stick) butter, melted

Preheat the oven to 250 degrees. Beat the egg white in a large bowl until frothy. Add the water, sugar, salt, allspice, cinnamon and cloves and mix well. Let stand for 15 minutes. Add the pecans and toss well to coat. Divide the butter between 2 baking sheets or sheet pans, spreading to coat the pans. Divide the pecan mixture between the pans and spread evenly. Bake for 1 hour. Remove from the oven and stir to loosen the pecans; cool. Store in an airtight container.

Makes about 4 cups

Party Mix with a Kick

4	cups corn Chex cereal
4	cups rice Chex cereal
4	cups wheat Chex cereal
2	cups small cheese crackers
1	(16-ounce) can peanuts
1/4	cup (1/2 stick) butter
1/3	cup Texas Pete hot sauce
1	tablespoon curry powder
3	tablespoons olive oil
2	tablespoons Worcestershire sauce
1	tablespoon soy sauce
1	teaspoon kosher salt
1/2	teaspoon garlic powder

Preheat the oven to 250 degrees. Combine the cereals, crackers and peanuts in a large bowl and toss to combine. Melt the butter in a saucepan or in the microwave and stir in the hot sauce, curry powder, olive oil, Worcestershire sauce, soy sauce, salt and garlic powder until blended. Pour over the cereal mixture and toss gently. Spread in 2 shallow baking pans. Bake for 1 hour or until crisp, stirring every 10 minutes.

Makes about 16 cups

MISS BRILES' TEA PARTY

SOUTHERN TEA PUNCH

PARTY CUCUMBER SANDWICHES

PESTO PINWHEELS

CHEDDAR AND PECAN CHEESE BALLS

CHEDDAR CHEESE STARS

PARTY PECANS

PENNY'S CARAMEL CAKE

FUDGY CREAM CHEESE BROWNIES

SNOWBALLS

CITRUS ALMOND PUNCH

10   cups water
2   cups sugar
1   (12-ounce) can frozen orange
     juice concentrate
1   (6-ounce) can frozen
     lemonade concentrate
1   teaspoon almond extract
1   teaspoon vanilla extract
1   (2-liter) bottle lemon-lime soda, chilled

Bring the water to a boil in a large kettle.
Add the sugar, orange juice concentrate,
lemonade concentrate, almond extract and
vanilla and stir until dissolved; cool. Pour
into freezer-proof containers and freeze.
To serve, thaw the mixture until slushy
and pour into a punch bowl. Add the soda
and serve.

Serves about 25

HOT HOLIDAY PUNCH

9   cups pineapple juice
9   cups cranberry juice cocktail
4 1/2 cups water
1   cup packed brown sugar
1/2 teaspoon salt
4   cinnamon sticks
4 1/2 teaspoons whole cloves

Pour the pineapple juice, cranberry juice
cocktail, water, brown sugar and salt into
a 24-cup or larger electric coffee percolator.
Put the cinnamon sticks and cloves in the
coffee basket. Heat until the punch
percolates for 10 minutes. Serve warm.

Serves 20

Tip: *Alternatively, you may combine all of
the ingredients in a stockpot and boil for
10 minutes. Strain before serving. This can
be made ahead and refrigerated.*

CRANBERRY TEA

4   cups water
1/3   cup sugar
2   cinnamon sticks
10 whole cloves
4   regular-size tea bags
1   (12-ounce) can frozen cranberry
     juice concentrate
     Ice

Combine the water, sugar, cinnamon sticks
and cloves in a large saucepan and bring to
a boil. Place the tea bags in a heatproof
bowl and pour the boiling mixture over the
tea bags. Steep for 3 minutes; remove the
tea bags. Strain into a pitcher and discard
the spices. Stir in the cranberry juice
concentrate. Chill for 1 hour or longer.
Serve over ice.

Makes about 4 cups

SOUTHERN SWEETENED TEA

6   cups water
4   family-size tea bags
1   to 1 3/4 cups sugar, or to taste
     Lemon wedges (optional)

Bring 6 cups water to a boil in a saucepan.
Add the tea bags and boil for 1 minute.
Remove from the heat. Steep, covered, for
10 minutes. Remove the tea bags, squeezing
gently. Add the sugar and stir until dissolved.
Pour into a 1-gallon pitcher and add cold
water to measure 1 gallon. Serve over ice
and garnish with lemon wedges, if desired.

Makes 1 gallon

SOUTHERN TEA PUNCH

5   cups boiling water
5   regular-size tea bags
8   mint sprigs, crushed
1   cup sugar
1   (12-ounce) can frozen orange
     juice concentrate
1   (12-ounce) can frozen
     lemonade concentrate
6 1/2 cups water
     Ice
     Additional fresh mint sprigs (optional)
     Lemon slices (optional)

Pour the boiling water over the tea bags in
a heatproof bowl and add 8 mint sprigs.
Steep, covered, for 5 minutes. Add the sugar
and steep for 5 minutes longer. Remove the
tea bags. Strain into a pitcher and discard
the mint. Stir in the orange juice concentrate,
lemonade concentrate and 6 1/2 cups water;
chill. Serve over ice and garnish with mint
and lemon slices, if desired.

Makes about 12 cups

STRAWBERRY TEA SLUSH

2   cups boiling water
4   regular-size tea bags
1/2 cup confectioners' sugar
1 3/4 cups frozen unsweetened strawberries
1   (6-ounce) can frozen
     lemonade concentrate
1   cup ice cubes

Pour the boiling water over the tea bags
in a heatproof bowl. Steep, covered, for
5 minutes. Remove the tea bags. Chill for
1 hour. Process the tea and the remaining
ingredients in a blender until slushy.

Makes about 4 cups

MORAVIAN COFFEE

3 1/2 gallons water
1 1/2 pounds regular-grind coffee
1 1/2 pounds (3 cups) sugar
4   cups (1 quart) milk
4   cups (1 quart) half-and-half

Pour the water into a 50-cup or larger
electric coffee percolator and add the
coffee to the coffee basket. Brew using the
manufacturer's directions. After brewing,
add the sugar, milk and half-and-half
to the coffee.

Makes 50 servings

Wasabi Bloody Mary

1/2   cup fresh lime juice
4 1/2   teaspoons wasabi paste
          (Japanese horseradish)
6   cups vegetable juice cocktail
3   tablespoons Worcestershire sauce
1 1/4   teaspoons hot red pepper sauce
3/4   teaspoon salt
1 1/2   cups vodka
          Ice
          Pickled asparagus, green beans or okra
          (optional)

Combine the lime juice and wasabi paste
in a small bowl and whisk until combined.
Combine the wasabi mixture, vegetable juice
cocktail, Worcestershire sauce, hot sauce
and salt in a pitcher and stir; chill. Stir in
the vodka. Serve over ice and garnish with
the pickled asparagus, if desired.

Makes about 8 cups

Delicious Margaritas

1   (6-ounce) can frozen limeade
          concentrate, thawed
          Tequila
          Triple Sec
          Ice

Pour the limeade concentrate into a blender.
Fill the concentrate can with tequila and add
to the blender. Fill the can 1/3 full of Triple
Sec and add to the blender. Fill the blender
with ice and blend until slushy. Pour into
glasses and serve.

Makes about 4 cups

Tip: *To salt the rims of the glasses, pour a small
amount of Triple Sec onto a flat plate and pour
coarse salt onto a second flat plate. Dip the rim
of each glass into the Triple Sec and then into
the salt.*

CHOCOLATE MARTINI

1/4   cup vodka
2   tablespoons chocolate-flavor liqueur
1 1/2   teaspoons raspberry-flavor liqueur
6   ice cubes
      Dash of half-and-half (optional)
      Chocolate candy kiss, unwrapped

Combine the vodka, chocolate and raspberry liqueurs, ice and half-and-half in a martini shaker and cover. Shake until well chilled. Place the chocolate kiss in a well-chilled martini glass. Strain the vodka mixture into the glass. Serve immediately.

Makes 1 serving

Tip: *For a special presentation, pour a small amount of chocolate liqueur onto a flat plate. Stir together baking cocoa and confectioners' sugar on a second flat plate. Dip the rim of the martini glass in the liqueur and then in the cocoa mixture to coat the rim.*

SIMPLE SANGRIA

1   (750-milliliter) bottle red wine
1   cup sugar
1   cup orange juice
1   cup brandy
1   cup Triple Sec
1   apple, diced
1   pear, diced
2   cups lemon-lime soda, chilled
2   cups ice

Combine the wine, sugar, orange juice, brandy, Triple Sec, apple and pear in a large pitcher and stir well. Chill for 2 hours. Just before serving, stir in the lemon-lime soda and the ice.

Makes about 8 cups

Cantaloupe Soup

1 large or 2 small cantaloupes, chopped
  Juice of 1 lime
1/4 cup sugar
1 cup heavy cream or whipping cream
1/4 cup sugar
1/2 small whole nutmeg, finely grated
  Grated zest of 1 lime
  Lime twists (optional)
  Mint leaves (optional)

Combine the cantaloupe, lime juice and
1/4 cup sugar in a food processor and
process until smooth. Beat the cream,
1/4 cup sugar and the nutmeg in a mixing
bowl until thickened. Fold in the lime zest
gently. Add the cantaloupe mixture and mix
until blended. Do not overmix or the cream
will separate from the cantaloupe. Pour into
glass bowls. Chill for several hours before
serving. Garnish each serving with a lime
twist and a mint leaf, if desired.

Serves 4 to 6

*The photograph for this recipe appears on
page 28.*

Strawberry Soup

1 1/2 cups water
3/4 cup light-bodied red wine
1/4 cup sugar
2 tablespoons fresh lemon juice
1 cinnamon stick
1 quart strawberries, puréed
1/2 cup heavy cream or whipping cream
1/4 cup sour cream

Combine the water, wine, sugar, lemon
juice and cinnamon stick in a 4-quart
saucepan and bring to a boil. Boil for
15 minutes, stirring occasionally. Add the
strawberries and simmer over medium-low
heat for 10 minutes, stirring frequently.
Remove and discard the cinnamon stick. Let
stand until cool. Whip the cream in a bowl
until stiff peaks form. Add the sour cream
and mix gently. Fold into the strawberry
mixture. Serve at room temperature.

Makes 1 1/2 quarts

Cucumber Soup

1   large or 2 small cucumbers, peeled,
    seeded and finely chopped
1   small onion, sliced
1   (10-ounce) can cream of chicken soup
1   cup sour cream
    Salt and pepper to taste

Combine the cucumber, onion, soup, sour cream, salt and pepper in a food processor and process until blended. Chill in the refrigerator until ready to serve.

Serves 4

Mazie Froelich, President 1969–1970

Quick-and-Easy French Onion Soup

4   onions, thinly sliced
2   large garlic cloves, minced
6   tablespoons butter
     All-purpose flour
4   (10-ounce) cans beef consommé
2   consommé cans water
1/2 cup brandy
2   tablespoons butter
3   tablespoons olive oil
8   slices French bread
1 1/2 cups (6 ounces) shredded Swiss cheese

Cook the onions and garlic in 6 tablespoons butter in a large saucepan until the onions are soft but not brown, stirring occasionally. Sprinkle flour over the onions and mix well. Add 1 can of the beef consommé and 1 consommé can of water and bring the mixture to a boil, stirring constantly.
Stir in the remaining beef consommé, the remaining water and the brandy. Cook until the soup is smooth and steaming. Heat 2 tablespoons butter and the olive oil in a skillet. Add the bread and cook until browned on both sides. To serve, place 1 slice of bread in the bottom of each soup bowl. Pour the soup over the bread and sprinkle with the Swiss cheese. Serve immediately.

Serves 8

CREAMY POTATO SOUP

1 1/2 pounds potatoes, peeled and finely chopped
3   tablespoons finely chopped yellow onion
1/4   cup (1/2 stick) butter
3   tablespoons finely chopped celery
3   tablespoons finely chopped carrots
2   cups milk
1/2   cup beef broth
5   tablespoons grated Parmesan cheese
1   teaspoon salt, or to taste
2   tablespoons chopped fresh parsley

Combine the potatoes with water to cover in a large soup pot. Cover and bring to a moderate boil. Boil until the potatoes are tender. Purée the potatoes with the cooking liquid in a food processor. Pour the mixture back into the soup pot.

Sauté the onion in the butter in a skillet until the onion is pale golden brown. Add the celery and carrots and cook for 2 minutes or until tender-crisp, stirring frequently. Add the onion mixture to the potatoes. Stir in the milk, beef broth and Parmesan cheese and simmer over medium heat for a few minutes or until the mixture is blended and creamy. Season with the salt. Add equal parts of additional broth and milk if the soup is too thick. Sprinkle with the parsley.

Serves 4 to 6

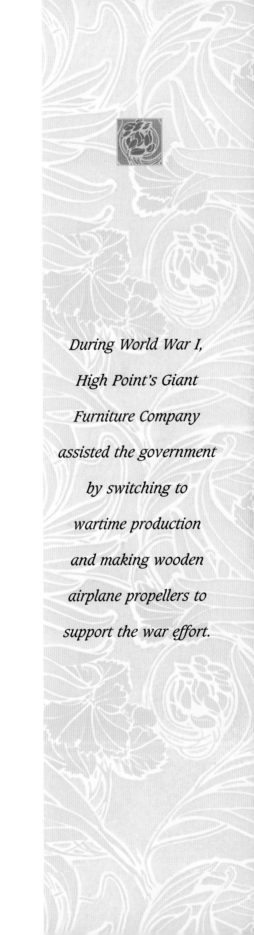

During World War I, High Point's Giant Furniture Company assisted the government by switching to wartime production and making wooden airplane propellers to support the war effort.

Sweet Red Pepper Soup

3 1/2 cups chopped onions
2   teaspoons olive oil
9   large red bell peppers, chopped
3   (10-ounce) cans no-salt-added
       chicken broth
1   tablespoon sherry vinegar
1/4   teaspoon salt
1/4   teaspoon pepper

Sauté the onions in the olive oil in a large
Dutch oven for 5 minutes or until tender.
Add the bell peppers and chicken broth
and bring to a boil. Reduce the heat and
simmer, covered, for 15 minutes. Process
the mixture in batches in a food processor
or blender until smooth. Return the mixture
to the Dutch oven. Add the vinegar, salt
and pepper and mix well. Cook over
medium-low heat until heated through.
Garnish each serving with fresh chives and
edible flowers.

Serves 8

Zucchini Soup

3   pounds zucchini, coarsely chopped
4   cups (or more) chicken stock
5   slices bacon, crisp-cooked, drained
       and chopped
1/3   cup minced fresh parsley
1   garlic clove, pressed
1 1/2 teaspoons dried basil
       Salt and freshly ground pepper to taste
       Paprika
4   to 6 teaspoons dry sherry (optional)

Combine the zucchini, chicken stock,
bacon, parsley, garlic, basil, salt and pepper
in a large saucepan and bring to a boil.
Reduce the heat and simmer for 15 minutes
or until the zucchini is tender, stirring
occasionally. Purée the mixture in batches
in a food processor or blender, adding
additional stock if the mixture is too thick.
Pour into a large bowl and let stand until
cool. Store, covered, in the refrigerator
until well chilled. Ladle into soup bowls.
Sprinkle with paprika and stir sherry into
each serving.

Serves 4 to 6

Slow-Cooker Vegetable Chili

1	zucchini, cut into 1/2-inch pieces
1	green bell pepper, coarsely chopped
1/2	cup coarsely chopped celery
1/2	cup coarsely chopped onion
2	garlic cloves, minced
2	to 3 teaspoons chili powder
1	teaspoon oregano
1/2	teaspoon cumin
2	(14-ounce) cans Mexican-style stewed tomatoes
1	(17-ounce) can whole kernel corn
1	(15-ounce) can black beans, drained and rinsed
1	(8-ounce) jar salsa
	Sour cream (optional)

Combine the zucchini, bell pepper, celery, onion, garlic, chili powder, oregano and cumin in a 3 1/2- or 4-quart slow cooker. Stir in the undrained tomatoes, undrained corn, black beans and salsa. Cook, covered, on Low for 8 to 10 hours or on High for 4 to 5 hours. Top each serving with sour cream, if desired.

Serves 4

Kim Heiman, President 2003–2004

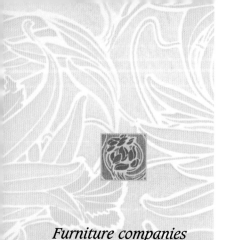

Furniture companies originally marketed their products through catalogs or by sending salesmen on the road with miniature samples. They began developing the idea of the showroom in the early twentieth century. However, the first attempts at furniture shows were not very successful.

Fireside Vegetable Soup

2	pounds stew beef
5	ribs celery, chopped
2	carrots, finely chopped
1	onion, sliced
1	bay leaf
1	envelope onion soup mix
1	(46-ounce) can vegetable juice cocktail
5	potatoes, chopped
1/2	head cabbage, chopped (optional)
1	(10-ounce) package frozen corn
1	(10-ounce) package frozen baby lima beans
1	(10-ounce) package peas
1	(16-ounce) can green beans
1	(15-ounce) can chopped tomatoes
2	tablespoons Worcestershire sauce
1/2	teaspoon Tabasco sauce
	Salt and pepper to taste

Brown the beef in a large stockpot. Add the celery, carrots, onion, bay leaf, soup mix and vegetable juice cocktail and mix well. Simmer, covered, for 3 hours, stirring occasionally. Add the potatoes, cabbage, corn, lima beans, peas, green beans, tomatoes, Worcestershire sauce, Tabasco sauce, salt and pepper. Simmer, uncovered, for 1 to 2 hours. Remove the bay leaf before serving.

Serves 12 to 15

Vegetable Beef Soup

1   pound extra-lean beef, trimmed
    and chopped
2   ribs celery, chopped
1   onion, chopped
2   (28-ounce) cans diced tomatoes
2   (10-ounce) packages frozen
    mixed vegetables
1   (8-ounce) can white corn, drained
2   potatoes, peeled and chopped
2   tablespoons chopped fresh parsley
1   tablespoon Accent
    Sugar to taste
    Salt and pepper to taste
1/2 cup barley

Cook the beef, celery and onion in water to cover in a Dutch oven for 30 minutes, stirring occasionally. Add the undrained tomatoes and cook for 30 minutes longer, stirring occasionally. Add the mixed vegetables, corn, potatoes, parsley and Accent and mix well. Season with sugar, salt and pepper. Cook for 30 minutes or until the vegetables are tender, adding the barley during the last 15 minutes. Add additional water if the soup becomes too thick.

Serves 6

Bootsy Tucker, President 1971–1972

Two-Timer Chicken Stew and Soup

1	(3-pound) chicken
	Salt to taste
1/4	cup (1/2 stick) butter or margarine
3	ribs celery, sliced
1	large onion, chopped
2	cups chicken broth
3	potatoes, peeled and quartered
1	tablespoon Worcestershire sauce
1	bay leaf
1 1/2	teaspoons salt, or to taste
1/2	teaspoon paprika
1/4	teaspoon pepper
1/4	teaspoon thyme
1	(16-ounce) can tomatoes
1	(16-ounce) can whole kernel corn, drained

Boil the chicken in salted water to cover in a stockpot until cooked through. Remove from the heat and let stand until cool. Remove the meat from the bones. Discard the bones and coarsely chop the meat. Melt the butter in a large stockpot. Add the celery and onion and cook until the vegetables are tender and golden brown, stirring frequently. Add the chicken broth, potatoes, Worcestershire sauce, bay leaf, 1 1/2 teaspoons salt, paprika, pepper, thyme and cooked chicken and simmer for 45 minutes, stirring occasionally. Add the undrained tomatoes and corn and simmer for 15 minutes, stirring occasionally. Remove the bay leaf. Serve as a main course. There will be enough left to serve a second time as a soup. Cut the chicken into smaller pieces and add more chicken broth if needed.

Serves 6

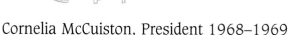

Cornelia McCuiston, President 1968–1969

White Bean Chili

2   tablespoons olive oil
2   large boneless skinless chicken breasts, finely chopped
1   onion, chopped
1   garlic clove, minced
2   chicken bouillon cubes
1 1/2 cups boiling water
1   cup cooked white navy beans
1   cup cooked Great Northern beans
1   (11-ounce) can white Shoe Peg corn, drained
2   (4-ounce) cans chopped green chiles, drained
1   teaspoon cumin
1   teaspoon salt

Heat the olive oil in a large saucepan over medium-high heat. Add the chicken, onion and garlic and sauté until the chicken is cooked through. Dissolve the bouillon cubes in the water in a small bowl. Add to the chicken mixture. Add the navy beans, Great Northern beans, corn, green chiles, cumin and salt and bring to a boil. Reduce the heat and simmer for 30 minutes, stirring occasionally.

Serves 4 to 6

Chicken Corn Chowder

3   chicken breasts
4   ribs celery, chopped
1   onion, chopped
6   cups water
3   (10-ounce) cans reduced-fat cream of chicken soup
3   (15-ounce) cans corn
3   (12-ounce) cans nonfat evaporated milk
16 slices American cheese
1   (2-ounce) jar pimentos
     Crushed red pepper flakes
     Tabasco sauce

Combine the chicken, celery, onion and water in a stockpot and bring to a boil. Boil until the chicken is cooked through. Remove the chicken and cut into pieces, reserving the broth. Add the chicken soup, corn and evaporated milk to the reserved broth. Add the chicken and bring the mixture to a simmer. Add the cheese 1 slice at a time, stirring until melted. Stir in the pimentos. Add red pepper flakes and Tabasco sauce to taste.

Serves 12

Simple Clam Chowder

2 pints half-and-half
4 (6-ounce) cans minced clams
1 slice bacon, chopped
4 small potatoes, finely chopped
1 onion, finely chopped

Combine the half-and-half, clams, bacon, potatoes and onion in a saucepan and bring to a boil. Reduce the heat and simmer for 1 1/2 hours, stirring occasionally.

Serves 4 to 6

Nancy Laney, President 1986–1987

Five-Cup Fruit Salad

1 cup mandarin oranges
1 cup crushed pineapple
1 cup sour cream
1 cup miniature marshmallows
1 cup flaked coconut

Combine all the ingredients in a bowl and mix gently. Chill, covered, until ready to serve.

Serves 6 to 8

Strawberry Gelatin Salad

1 (3-ounce) package strawberry gelatin
1 1/2 cups boiling water
1/2 (15-ounce) can crushed pineapple
1 (8-ounce) package frozen strawberries
1 to 2 cups sour cream
1/2 cup chopped pecans
1 banana, mashed, or more to taste

Dissolve the gelatin in the boiling water in a bowl. Add the pineapple and strawberries and mix well. Pour into a gelatin mold. Chill in the refrigerator for 5 to 6 hours. Mix the remaining ingredients in a bowl. Spread over the gelatin mixture. Chill for 1 hour.

Serves 8 to 10

Apricot Salad Delicious

2   cups apricot nectar
1   (3-ounce) package lemon gelatin
2   (3-ounce) packages orange gelatin
1   (20-ounce) can crushed pineapple
1   (11-ounce) can mandarin oranges
2   bananas, mashed
2   eggs, beaten
1/4   cup sugar
1/4   cup lemon juice
    Grated zest of 1 lemon
1/2   pint heavy cream or whipping cream, whipped and sweetened to taste
    Shredded cheese

Heat the nectar in a saucepan. Stir in the gelatins. Drain the pineapple and mandarin oranges, reserving the liquid. Add enough water to the reserved liquid to measure 4 cups. Stir into the gelatin mixture and cool. Stir in the pineapple, mandarin oranges and bananas. Pour into a serving dish. Chill until the gelatin is set. Combine the eggs, sugar, lemon juice and lemon zest in a saucepan over medium heat. Cook until thickened, stirring constantly. Remove from the heat and cool. Fold in the whipped cream. Spread over the congealed salad. Sprinkle with cheese. Chill until ready to serve.

Serves 12 to 14

Frozen Banana Salad

2   bananas, chopped
1   (8-ounce) can crushed pineapple, drained
2   cups sour cream
2/3   cup sugar
1   cup chopped pecans
    Lettuce leaves

Combine the bananas, pineapple, sour cream, sugar and pecans in a bowl and mix gently. Spoon into a freezer-proof container. Store, covered, in the freezer until frozen. Remove from the freezer 15 minutes before serving. Cut into squares and serve on lettuce leaves.

Serves 4 to 6

Odelle Marsh, President 1940–1942

Frozen Cranberry Salad

1   (16-ounce) can jellied cranberry sauce
3   tablespoons lemon juice
1   cup heavy cream or whipping
     cream, whipped
1/4 cup mayonnaise
1/4 cup confectioners' sugar
1   cup chopped walnuts
     Lettuce leaves

Mash the cranberry sauce in a bowl. Add the lemon juice and mix well. Spoon into fluted paper cups placed in muffin cups. Place in the freezer. Combine the whipped cream, mayonnaise, confectioners' sugar and walnuts in a bowl and mix well. Spoon over the cranberry layer. Freeze until firm. Remove from the paper cups and serve on lettuce leaves.

Serves 6 to 8

Bluegrass Salad

1/2 cup vegetable oil
1/4 cup rice vinegar
1   tablespoon balsamic vinegar
2   tablespoons sugar
1   teaspoon butter or margarine
3/4 cup walnuts
2   heads romaine, torn
2   pears, chopped
1   cup asparagus tips, broccoli florets or
     snow peas
1/2 cup crumbled blue cheese
1/2 cup dried cranberries

Combine the oil, rice vinegar, balsamic vinegar and sugar in a bowl and whisk until blended. Chill, covered, for 1 hour or longer. Melt the butter in a skillet over medium heat. Add the walnuts and sauté for 5 minutes or until lightly browned. Remove the walnuts with a slotted spoon. Combine the romaine, pears, asparagus tips and walnuts in a bowl and toss gently. Sprinkle with the blue cheese and cranberries. Drizzle with the dressing.

Serves 6 to 8

Strawberry Blue Salad

CHILI-SWEET PECANS

1/4 cup sugar
1 cup warm water
1 cup pecan halves
2 tablespoons sugar
1 tablespoon chili powder
1/8 teaspoon ground red pepper

BALSAMIC VINAIGRETTE

1/2 cup balsamic vinegar
3 tablespoons Dijon mustard
3 tablespoons honey
2 garlic cloves, minced
2 small shallots, minced
1/4 teaspoon salt
1/4 teaspoon pepper
1 cup olive oil

SALAD

1 pound mixed salad greens, torn
4 ounces blue cheese, crumbled
2 oranges, peeled and thinly sliced
1 pint strawberries, quartered

For the pecans, combine 1/4 cup sugar and the water in a bowl and stir until the sugar dissolves. Add the pecans and let stand for 10 minutes. Drain and discard the sugar mixture. Preheat the oven to 350 degrees. Combine 2 tablespoons sugar, the chili powder and red pepper. Add the pecans and toss to coat. Spread on a greased baking sheet. Bake for 10 minutes or until the pecans are brown, stirring once.

For the vinaigrette, combine the vinegar, Dijon mustard, honey, garlic, shallots, salt and pepper in a bowl and whisk until blended. Add the olive oil gradually, whisking constantly.

For the salad, toss the salad greens with the vinaigrette and blue cheese in a large bowl. Place on individual salad plates. Arrange the oranges and strawberries over the top. Sprinkle with the pecans.

Serves 4 to 6

The photograph for this recipe appears on page 28.

Spinach Salad with Oranges and Tomatoes

FRENCH DRESSING
1/2 cup ketchup
1/2 cup canola oil or olive oil
1 tablespoon apple cider vinegar
1 teaspoon lemon juice
1 teaspoon Worcestershire sauce
2 tablespoons sugar
Dash of salt
Dash of pepper

SALAD
1 (10-ounce) bag baby spinach leaves or mixed salad greens
1 (15-ounce) can mandarin oranges, drained
1/2 pint cherry tomatoes or grape tomatoes
Sliced almonds

For the dressing, combine the ketchup, canola oil, vinegar, lemon juice, Worcestershire sauce, sugar, salt and pepper in a jar with a tight-fitting lid and shake until blended.

For the salad, combine the spinach, oranges, tomatoes and almonds in a bowl. Drizzle with the salad dressing and toss gently.

Serves 6

Mixed Greens and Fruit with Red Wine Vinaigrette

RED WINE VINAIGRETTE
2 tablespoons olive oil
2 tablespoons red wine vinegar
2 garlic cloves, minced
1/8 teaspoon salt

SALAD
1/2 head romaine, torn
1/2 head butter lettuce, torn
1/2 bunch leaf lettuce, torn
1 (11-ounce) can mandarin oranges, drained
1 cup seedless red grapes
1/2 cup slivered toasted almonds

For the vinaigrette, combine the olive oil, vinegar, garlic and salt in a bowl and whisk until blended.

For the salad, combine the romaine, butter lettuce, leaf lettuce, oranges, grapes and almonds in a bowl. Drizzle with the vinaigrette and toss gently.

Serves 6 to 8

Black Bean and Corn Salad

SOUTHWESTERN VINAIGRETTE

1/3 cup chopped fresh cilantro
1/2 cup lime juice
1/2 cup olive oil
1/2 cup sour cream
1   teaspoon sugar
1/2 teaspoon salt
1/2 teaspoon pepper

SALAD

1   (12-ounce) package romaine, shredded
5   plum tomatoes, chopped
1   (15-ounce) can black beans, rinsed and drained
1   small purple onion, chopped
2   cups (8 ounces) shredded Mexican four-cheese blend
2   (7-ounce) cans whole kernel corn with red and green
     peppers, drained
2   (4-ounce) cans sliced black olives, drained
2   cups crushed tortilla chips
     Fresh cilantro leaves

For the vinaigrette, combine the cilantro, lime juice, olive oil, sour cream, sugar, salt and pepper in a blender or food processor and process until smooth.

For the salad, layer the romaine, tomatoes, black beans, onion, cheese, corn, olives and tortilla chips in a large glass bowl. Pour the vinaigrette over the salad just before serving and toss gently. Garnish with cilantro leaves. Serve immediately.

Serves 6 to 8

In 1919, the Southern Furniture Exposition Company began constructing a permanent ten-story building on South Main Street. It was the first building in High Point built specifically to house showroom space. Previously, showrooms were located in empty commercial spaces.

Garden Pea Salad with Bacon and Cheese

6   tablespoons mayonnaise
      Juice of 1 lemon
1   small white onion, finely chopped, or
      2 tablespoons minced chives
2   cups frozen garden peas
1   cup (4 ounces) Swiss cheese or
      Cheddar cheese strips
      Salt and pepper to taste
2   cups torn lettuce
8   slices bacon, crisp-cooked and
      crumbled

Combine the mayonnaise, lemon juice,
onion, peas and cheese in a bowl and mix
gently. Season with salt and pepper. Chill,
covered, for 8 to 10 hours. Add the lettuce
and bacon and toss gently. Adjust the
seasonings to taste. Serve immediately.

Serves 6

Layered Vegetable Salad

1/2   head romaine
6   hard-cooked eggs, sliced
1   cup (4 ounces) shredded Swiss cheese
1   pound fresh spinach, torn
1   (10-ounce) package frozen tiny
      English peas, thawed and drained
1   small red onion, thinly sliced and
      separated into rings
6   to 12 slices bacon, crisp-cooked
      and crumbled
1   cup regular or light mayonnaise
1   cup Italian salad dressing made with
      balsamic vinegar
1   teaspoon sugar
1   cup (4 ounces) shredded sharp
      Cheddar cheese

Arrange the lettuce in a 9×13-inch dish.
Layer the eggs, 1/4 cup of the Swiss cheese,
the spinach, 1/4 cup of the Swiss cheese,
the peas, 1/4 cup of the Swiss cheese, the
onion, the remaining 1/4 cup Swiss cheese
and the bacon over the lettuce. Combine the
mayonnaise, salad dressing and sugar in a
bowl and mix well. Spread over the salad,
sealing to the edge of the dish. Sprinkle
with the Cheddar cheese. Chill, covered
tightly, for several hours or overnight.
Cut into squares to serve.

Serves 8 to 10

Eternal Slaw

1   large head cabbage
1   carrot
3/4   cup sugar
1   teaspoon salt
1   cup vinegar
1/2   cup vegetable oil
2   teaspoons celery seeds
1   tablespoon sugar

Chop the cabbage in a food processor. Add the carrot, 3/4 cup sugar and the salt and pulse to chop the carrot. Spoon the mixture into a bowl. Combine the vinegar, oil, celery seeds and 1 tablespoon sugar in a small saucepan over low heat. Heat until the sugar is dissolved, stirring frequently. Pour over the cabbage mixture and toss to combine. Chill, covered, until ready to serve.

Serves 8 to 10

Black-Eyed Pea Salad

2   (15-ounce) cans black-eyed peas, drained
1   cup chopped red onion
1   cup chopped green bell pepper
1   garlic clove, minced
1   cup apple cider vinegar
1   cup canola oil
1   cup sugar
1   teaspoon salt
     Dash of pepper
     Dash of hot red pepper sauce

Combine the black-eyed peas, onion, bell pepper and garlic in a bowl and toss gently. Combine the vinegar, canola oil, sugar, salt, pepper and hot sauce in a bowl and whisk until blended and the sugar is dissolved. Pour over the pea mixture. Chill, covered, for 12 hours or longer.

Serves 6

Tip: For a variation, add corn, lima beans, or your favorite beans.

Broccoli Salad

2   bunches broccoli florets
1   small purple onion, chopped
1/2   cup raisins
1/2   cup mayonnaise
2   tablespoons vinegar (preferably
    rice vinegar)
2   teaspoons sugar
12   slices bacon, crisp-cooked
    and crumbled

Combine the broccoli, onion and raisins in a bowl and toss gently. Combine the mayonnaise, vinegar and sugar in a bowl and mix well. Pour over the broccoli mixture and toss gently to coat. Chill, covered, for 2 hours. Sprinkle the bacon over the top just before serving.

Serves 8 to 10

Artichoke Potato Salad

1   (14-ounce) can artichoke hearts,
    drained and finely chopped
1   pound red potatoes, cooked, peeled
    and finely chopped
1   bunch green onions, chopped
3   ribs celery, chopped
3   garlic cloves, minced
1   cup mayonnaise
2   teaspoons Dijon mustard
3   tablespoons chopped fresh chervil
2   tablespoons chopped fresh dill weed
1   tablespoon chopped fresh parsley
    Juice of 1/2 lemon
1   tablespoon sugar
    Salt to taste
    Freshly ground pepper to taste

Combine the artichoke hearts and potatoes in a bowl and toss gently. Combine the green onions, celery, garlic, mayonnaise, Dijon mustard, chervil, dill weed, parsley, lemon juice and sugar in a large bowl and mix well. Add the potato mixture and stir gently. Season with salt and pepper. Chill, covered, for several hours before serving.

Serves 6 to 8

Potato Salad

2 1/4 pounds new red potatoes
1/2 cup chopped celery
1/2 small Vidalia onion, finely
    chopped (optional)
3 eggs, hard-cooked and finely chopped
1 cup sweet pickle relish
1/4 cup chopped pimento-stuffed
    green olives
1/2 cup mayonnaise, or to taste
    Salt and pepper to taste

Combine the unpeeled potatoes with water to cover in a stockpot and bring to a simmer. Simmer for 15 minutes or just until tender. Drain and run cold water over the potatoes to cool. Peel the cooled potatoes, if desired, and cut into 1-inch pieces. Combine the potatoes with the celery, onion, eggs, pickle relish, green olives, mayonnaise, salt and pepper in a large bowl and mix gently. Chill, covered, until ready to serve.

Serves 8 to 10

Cucumber Congealed Salad

1 package lime gelatin
1 cup boiling water
1/4 cup vinegar
1 onion, grated
1 cup mayonnaise
1 large cucumber, shredded
    Lettuce

Combine the gelatin, water, vinegar, onion, mayonnaise, and cucumber in a bowl and mix well. Spoon into 8 individual-size gelatin molds. Chill until firm. Serve over lettuce.

Serves 8

Veggies Dilled and Chilled

1   (16-ounce) can French-style green beans, rinsed and drained

1   (16-ounce) can white corn, rinsed and drained

1   (16-ounce) can small early peas, rinsed and drained

1   (4-ounce) can sliced mushrooms, drained

1 1/2 cups chopped cauliflower

1/2   cup chopped onion

1/4   cup chopped green bell pepper

1   cup sugar

3/4   cup vinegar

1/2   cup vegetable oil

1   tablespoon water

1/2   teaspoon dill weed

1   teaspoon salt

1/2   teaspoon pepper

Combine the green beans, corn, peas, mushrooms, cauliflower, onion and bell pepper in a large bowl. Whisk together the sugar, vinegar, oil, water, dill weed, salt and pepper in a bowl until blended. Pour over the vegetables and toss to coat. Store, covered, in the refrigerator until thoroughly chilled.

Serves about 16

Eva Dell Marsh, President 1978–1979

ORZO SALAD

1 1/2 cups orzo

10 kalamata olives, sliced

4 green onions, thinly sliced

2 ribs celery, thinly sliced

1 red bell pepper, thinly sliced

1 zucchini, finely chopped

1/2 cup minced fresh parsley

1/3 cup olive oil

2 tablespoons red wine vinegar

3 garlic cloves, minced

1 tablespoon dried dill weed

1 teaspoon dried oregano

1/4 teaspoon salt

1/8 teaspoon pepper

4 ounces feta cheese, crumbled

2 tablespoons mayonnaise

Cook the orzo using the package directions. Drain and rinse with cold water. Combine the orzo, olives, green onions, celery, bell pepper, zucchini and parsley in a large bowl and mix well. Combine the olive oil, vinegar, garlic, dill weed, oregano, salt and pepper in a bowl and whisk until blended. Pour over the orzo mixture. Sprinkle with the cheese and toss gently to coat. Stir in the mayonnaise. Chill, covered, for 2 hours or longer. Bring to room temperature before serving.

Serves 8

The photograph for this recipe appears on page 78.

Ginger Beef Salad

GINGER DRESSING
2   tablespoons vegetable oil
2   tablespoons cider vinegar
1   tablespoon sugar
1   teaspoon finely grated ginger
    Pepper to taste

SALAD
8   ounces steak or roast beef, cooked rare
    and thinly sliced
4   ounces vermicelli, broken into 3-inch
    pieces, cooked and cooled
1   cup halved pea pods
1   cup shredded red cabbage
1/2 cup very thinly sliced carrot
1/2 cup sliced green onions
1   (8-ounce) can sliced water
    chestnuts, drained

For the dressing, combine the oil, vinegar,
sugar, ginger and pepper in a jar with a
tight-fitting lid and shake until blended or
whisk together in a bowl.

For the salad, combine the steak, vermicelli,
pea pods, cabbage, carrot, green onions and
water chestnuts in a large bowl. Pour the
dressing over the salad and toss gently to
coat. Chill, covered, for 1 hour or longer
before serving.

Serves 4

Chinese Chicken Salad

3   to 4 cups chopped cooked
    chicken breasts
1   head iceberg lettuce or romaine, or a
    combination of both, chopped into
    bite-size pieces
3   green onions, chopped
1   (2-ounce) package slivered
    almonds, toasted
1   (15-ounce) can mandarin
    oranges, drained
2   tablespoons poppy seeds
1/2 cup vegetable oil
1/4 cup cider vinegar
1/4 cup sugar
2   teaspoons salt
1/2 teaspoon pepper
1   (5-ounce) can chow mein noodles

Combine the chicken, lettuce, green onions,
almonds, mandarin oranges and poppy
seeds in a bowl. Combine the oil, vinegar,
sugar, salt and pepper in a bowl and whisk
until blended and the sugar is dissolved.
Pour over the salad and toss gently to coat.
Add the noodles and toss gently.

Serves 4 to 6

Seacoast Salad

1	cup seashell pasta
1	cucumber, chopped
1/4	cup finely chopped red onion
10	ounces imitation crab meat or boiled and peeled shrimp, or a combination of both
2/3	cup mayonnaise
2	tablespoons vegetable oil
2	tablespoons white wine vinegar
1	teaspoon salt
1/4	teaspoon (or more) dill weed
1/8	teaspoon pepper

Cook the pasta using the package directions; drain. Combine the warm pasta, cucumber, red onion and crab meat in a bowl. Combine the mayonnaise, oil, vinegar, salt, dill weed and pepper in a bowl and mix until blended. Pour over the pasta mixture and toss to coat. Chill, covered, for 30 minutes before serving.

Serves 6 to 8

Overnight Shrimp Salad

1	head lettuce, shredded
1	bunch green onions, chopped
1	(8-ounce) can water chestnuts, drained and chopped
1	(10-ounce) package frozen peas
1	bunch radishes, chopped
2	pounds small shrimp, cooked and peeled
3	or 4 ribs celery, chopped
1 1/2	cups Miracle Whip salad dressing
1	tablespoon sugar
2	cups (8 ounces) shredded Swiss cheese
3	hard-cooked eggs, finely chopped

Layer the lettuce, green onions, water chestnuts, peas, radishes, shrimp and celery in a large glass bowl. Spread the Miracle Whip over the top. Sprinkle with the sugar. Chill, covered, for 8 to 10 hours. Sprinkle with the cheese and eggs just before serving.

Serves 6 to 8

Margaret Lewis, President 1991–1992

Tropical Spinach Salad with Grilled Shrimp

2   pounds fresh large shrimp or
     2 (1-pound) pork tenderloins or
     6 boneless skinless chicken breasts
1   bottle favorite citrus marinade
12   (12-inch) wooden skewers
2   (6-ounce) packages fresh baby spinach
2   mangoes, sliced
1   red onion, sliced
1   (3-ounce) package goat
     cheese, crumbled
1   cup fresh raspberries
1/2 cup chopped pistachio nuts
1   bottle favorite vinaigrette

Peel and devein the shrimp and place in a large sealable plastic bag. Add the citrus marinade and shake to coat. Chill for 1 hour. Soak the skewers in water to cover for 30 minutes. Remove the shrimp from the marinade and discard the marinade. Thread the shrimp onto the skewers. Grill the shrimp with the grill lid down over medium-high heat for 2 minutes on each side or until the shrimp turn pink. Remove the shrimp from the skewers.

Arrange the spinach on a large serving platter. Top with the mangoes, onion and shrimp. Sprinkle with the goat cheese, raspberries and pistachio nuts. Serve with the vinaigrette.

To prepare the pork, marinate as directed above. Grill with the grill lid down over medium-high heat for 10 to 12 minutes on each side or until a meat thermometer inserted into the thickest portion of the meat registers 155 degrees. Let stand for 10 minutes before slicing.

To prepare the chicken, marinate as directed above. Grill with the grill lid down over medium-high heat for 4 minutes on each side or until cooked through. Let stand for 10 minutes before slicing.

Serves 6

Shrimp and Vermicelli Salad

1	pound vermicelli, cooked
3	tablespoons lemon juice
3	tablespoons vegetable oil
	Seasoned salt to taste
2	pounds shrimp, cleaned and cooked
1	green bell pepper, chopped
1	cup chopped celery
1	cup black olives, drained and sliced
1	to 1 1/2 cups mayonnaise
1/2	teaspoon hot red pepper sauce
	Salt, pepper and garlic salt to taste

Combine the vermicelli, lemon juice and oil in a bowl and mix well. Sprinkle generously with seasoned salt. Chill, covered, for 24 hours. Combine the shrimp, bell pepper, celery, black olives, mayonnaise, hot sauce, salt, pepper and garlic salt in a bowl and mix well. Add to the pasta mixture and toss. Serve chilled.

Serves 18 to 20

Martha Amos, President 1961–1962

Cooked Dressing for Chicken Salad

3/4	cup milk
1/4	cup vinegar
1	egg, well beaten
1	tablespoon all-purpose flour
1	tablespoon sugar
1	teaspoon salt
1	teaspoon dry mustard
	Dash of red pepper flakes

Combine the milk, vinegar, egg, flour, sugar, salt, dry mustard and red pepper flakes in a saucepan over low heat. Cook until thickened, stirring frequently. Combine with chopped cooked chicken, adding Miracle Whip if the mixture is too dry.

Makes about 1 1/4 cups dressing

CRANBERRY BALSAMIC VINAIGRETTE

1/2   cup whole cranberry sauce
3/4   cup vegetable oil
1/4   cup balsamic vinegar
1/4   teaspoon salt
1/8   teaspoon pepper

Combine the cranberry sauce, oil, vinegar, salt and pepper in a food processor or blender and process until smooth. Store in the refrigerator until ready to use.

Makes about 1 cup

FRESH LEMON VINAIGRETTE

1/4   cup fresh lemon juice
1   large garlic clove, pressed
1   teaspoon Dijon mustard
1/4   teaspoon salt
1/4   teaspoon freshly ground pepper
1/2   cup olive oil

Whisk together the lemon juice, garlic, Dijon mustard, salt and pepper in a bowl. Add the olive oil gradually, whisking constantly until blended. Store, tightly covered, in the refrigerator for up to 1 week. Bring to room temperature and whisk before serving.

Makes about 3/4 cup

ROQUEFORT SALAD DRESSING

3/4 cup vegetable oil
3   tablespoons vinegar
3   tablespoons sugar
1   teaspoon fresh onion juice
4   ounces Roquefort cheese

Combine the oil, vinegar, sugar, onion juice and cheese in a blender and process until smooth. Serve with vegetable salads or fruit salads.

Makes about 1 1/2 cups

Elizabeth "Bonie" Wall, President 1946–1947

SESAME SALAD DRESSING

1   tablespoon green peppercorn mustard
     or Dijon mustard
1   tablespoon balsamic vinegar
1   tablespoon raspberry vinegar
1   teaspoon honey
     Salt and freshly ground pepper
3   tablespoons Asian sesame oil
     Toasted sesame seeds (optional)

Combine the peppercorn mustard, balsamic vinegar, raspberry vinegar, honey, salt and pepper in a bowl and whisk until blended. Add the sesame oil gradually, whisking constantly. Chill until ready to use. Toss with salad greens and sprinkle with sesame seeds.

Makes about 1/3 cup

CENTERPIECES

MEAT

POULTRY

SEAFOOD

&

PASTA

Sesame Lamb Chops *page 88*
Roasted Vegetables *page 136*
Orzo Salad *page 71*

Easy Stroganoff

1   (10-ounce) can onion soup
1/2   (10-ounce) can cream of
      mushroom soup
1 1/2 pounds beef stew cubes, trimmed
2   cups sour cream, at room temperature
1   (8-ounce) can sliced buttered
      mushrooms, drained
12   to 16 ounces egg noodles, cooked

Preheat the oven to 250 degrees. Combine
the onion soup and mushroom soup in
a bowl and mix well. Stir in the beef.
Spoon into a large deep baking dish. Bake,
covered, for 4 hours. Remove from the oven
and stir in the sour cream and mushrooms.
Let stand, covered, for 10 minutes. Serve
over the noodles.

Serves 4 to 6

Beef with Peppers and Rice

1   pound ground round
    Butter or vegetable oil
3/4 to 1 cup chopped onion
1   green bell pepper, chopped
1   (6-ounce) can tomato paste
2   tablespoons brown sugar
    Worcestershire sauce to taste
    Salt and pepper to taste
1   cup uncooked quick-cooking rice
1   (15-ounce) can whole tomatoes
1   cup water

Preheat the oven to 375 degrees. Brown
the beef in butter in a large skillet, stirring
until crumbly; drain. Add the onion and bell
pepper and cook until browned. Stir in the
tomato paste, brown sugar, Worcestershire
sauce, salt and pepper. Pour the mixture
into a 9×13-inch baking dish. Top evenly
with the rice. Pour the undrained tomatoes,
then the water evenly over the top,
moistening all the rice. Bake, covered,
for 1 hour.

Serves 6 to 8

DOUBLE-MEAT LASAGNA

SAUCE

2	pounds ground beef
1	pound sweet Italian sausage, casings removed
2	tablespoons olive oil
1	envelope onion soup mix
1	cup dry red wine
1	teaspoon ground allspice
2	(28-ounce) cans whole peeled tomatoes
1	(12-ounce) jar spaghetti sauce
1	(6-ounce) can tomato paste

LASAGNA

32	ounces ricotta cheese
1	(10-ounce) package frozen chopped spinach, thawed and squeezed dry
24	ounces mozzarella cheese, shredded
6	ounces Parmesan or Romano cheese, grated
16	ounces uncooked lasagna noodles
12	ounces provolone cheese, thinly sliced
1/4	cup water

For the sauce, brown the ground beef and sausage in the olive oil in a large saucepan, stirring until crumbly; drain. Stir in the soup mix, wine and allspice and simmer for 15 minutes. Add the undrained tomatoes, spaghetti sauce and tomato paste and mix well. Simmer for 30 minutes. Preheat the oven to 350 degrees.

For the lasagna, combine the ricotta cheese and spinach in a bowl and mix well. Spread a layer of the sauce in the bottom of a 10×18-inch lasagna pan. Top with a layer of the uncooked noodles, spinach mixture, provolone cheese, mozzarella cheese and Parmesan cheese. Repeat layering of the sauce, noodles, spinach mixture, provolone cheese, mozzarella cheese and Parmesan cheese until the pan is full, ending with the sauce and cheeses. Add 1/4 cup water around the edge of the pan. The mixture must be moist for the noodles to cook properly. Bake for 1 hour, covering the pan if the cheeses become too brown. Let stand for 20 minutes before cutting.

Serves 10

Susan Morris, President 1989–1990

Tip: *The lasagna can also be refrigerated, covered, overnight and then reheated.*

Classic Mini Meat Loaves

MEAT LOAVES

1 1/4   pounds meat loaf mix (beef, pork and veal) or ground beef

2   eggs

1/2   cup quick-cooking oats

1/2   cup ketchup

1/2   cup finely chopped onion

1/3   cup finely chopped bell pepper

1/3   cup minced parsley

1   tablespoon minced garlic

1   tablespoon Worcestershire sauce

1/2   teaspoon thyme

1/2   teaspoon salt

SAUCE

1/2   cup ketchup

1   tablespoon water

1   teaspoon Worcestershire sauce

For the meat loaves, preheat the oven to 350 degrees. Combine the meat, eggs, oats, ketchup, onion, bell pepper, parsley, garlic, Worcestershire sauce, thyme and salt in a large bowl. Mix well using your hands or a wooden spoon. Shape into four 2 1/2×5-inch loaves and place in a foil-lined baking pan. Bake for 20 to 25 minutes or until a meat thermometer inserted in the center of the loaves registers 160 degrees.

For the sauce, stir together the ketchup, water and Worcestershire sauce in a small bowl. Serve with the meat loaves.

Serves 4

Chips and Salsa Mini Meat Loaves

MEAT LOAVES

1 1/4 pounds meat loaf mix (beef, pork and veal) or ground beef
2 eggs
2/3 cup salsa
1/2 cup crushed tortilla chips
1/2 cup finely chopped onion
1/2 cup (2 ounces) shredded Cheddar cheese
1/4 cup chopped fresh cilantro
2 teaspoons chili powder
1/2 teaspoon salt

SAUCE

1/2 cup salsa
2 tablespoons chopped fresh cilantro

For the meat loaves, preheat the oven to 350 degrees. Combine the meat, eggs, salsa, tortilla chips, onion, cheese, cilantro, chili powder and salt in a large bowl. Mix well using your hands or a wooden spoon. Shape into four 2 1/2×5-inch loaves and place in a foil-lined baking pan. Bake for 20 minutes or until a meat thermometer inserted in the center registers 160 degrees.

For the sauce, stir together the salsa and cilantro in a small bowl. Serve with the meat loaves.

Serves 4

Asian Mini Meat Loaves

MEAT LOAVES

1 1/4 pounds meat loaf mix (beef, pork and veal) or ground beef
2 eggs
1 (8-ounce) can sliced water chestnuts, drained and chopped
1/3 to 1/2 cup hoisin or stir-fry sauce
1/3 cup dry bread crumbs
1/3 cup finely chopped bell pepper
1/3 cup sliced scallions
1 teaspoon minced garlic
1 teaspoon grated fresh ginger
1/2 teaspoon salt

SAUCE

1/2 cup hoisin or stir-fry sauce
2 tablespoons water
2 tablespoons sliced scallions

For the meat loaves, preheat the oven to 350 degrees. Combine all the ingredients in a large bowl and mix well using your hands or a wooden spoon. Shape into four 2 1/2×5-inch loaves and place in a foil-lined baking pan. Bake for 20 minutes or until a meat thermometer inserted in the center of the loaves registers 160 degrees.

For the sauce, stir together the hoisin sauce, water and scallions in a small bowl. Serve with the meat loaves.

Serves 4

Spaghetti Sauce

1	pound ground round
4	slices bacon, chopped
1	cup chopped onion
3	to 6 garlic cloves, chopped
3	to 4 tablespoons olive oil
2	(6-ounce) cans Italian tomato paste, or 6 tomatoes, seeded and chopped, or 2 (16-ounce) cans whole plum tomatoes
1/2	cup chopped celery
1/2	cup chopped bell pepper
1/2	cup chopped fresh parsley
1	tablespoon chopped fresh basil, or 1 teaspoon dried basil
1	tablespoon chopped fresh oregano, or 1 teaspoon dried oregano
1	bay leaf
1/8	teaspoon red pepper flakes
1	to 3 teaspoons sugar, or to taste
	Salt and pepper to taste

Brown the beef and bacon in a large skillet over medium heat, stirring until the beef is crumbly; drain. Sauté the onion and garlic in the olive oil in a stockpot over medium heat until tender. Add the meat and remaining ingredients and bring to a low boil. Cook, covered, over low heat for 2 hours, stirring occasionally. Remove the bay leaf. Serve over pasta immediately or chill, covered, for 1 to 2 days to allow the flavors to blend.

Serves about 8

Savory Meatballs

1	(15-ounce) can tomato sauce
3/4	cup water
1	teaspoon Worcestershire sauce
1/2	teaspoon sugar
1	egg
1	pound ground beef
1/4	cup uncooked rice
2	tablespoons finely chopped onion
1	teaspoon parsley flakes
1	teaspoon salt
1/8	teaspoon marjoram
	Dash of pepper

Combine the tomato sauce and water in a bowl. Remove and reserve 1/2 cup of the tomato sauce mixture. Add the Worcestershire sauce and sugar to the remaining tomato sauce mixture. Beat the egg in a large bowl and add the beef, rice, onion, parsley, salt, marjoram, pepper and reserved 1/2 cup tomato sauce mixture and mix well. Shape into 18 to 20 meatballs and place in a large skillet. Pour the remaining tomato sauce mixture over the meatballs. Bring to a boil. Reduce the heat and simmer, covered, for 35 to 40 minutes.

Serves 4 to 6

Skeen Burgers

5   pounds ground chuck
1   cup applesauce
1   cup crushed Ritz crackers
1   tablespoon Tabasco sauce
5   teaspoons Accent
5   teaspoons Worcestershire sauce
1   envelope onion soup mix
1/2   teaspoon garlic powder
    Salt to taste

Combine the beef, applesauce, crackers, Tabasco sauce, Accent, Worcestershire sauce, soup mix, garlic powder and salt in a large bowl and mix well using your hands. Shape into patties. Grill until cooked through, or wrap tightly and freeze for later use.

Makes 10 to 15 large burgers

Hot Dog Chili

1/2   pound ground round
1   (8-ounce) can tomato sauce
2   tablespoons ketchup
2   teaspoons minced dried onion
    Chili powder or other favorite seasoning to taste
1/2   teaspoon sugar

Brown the beef in a skillet, stirring until crumbly; drain. Add the tomato sauce, ketchup, onion, chili powder and sugar and mix well. Simmer to desired consistency. Spoon over hot dogs in buns.

Serves 6 to 8

Tip: *This chili can be doubled or tripled and can be frozen for later use.*

Osso Buco

1	tablespoon all-purpose flour
1/2	teaspoon pepper
1/4	teaspoon salt
2	to 2 1/2 pounds veal shanks, cut into 1 1/2-inch-thick pieces
1	tablespoon olive oil
1	cup minced carrots
1	cup minced celery
1	cup minced onion
1/2	cup minced green bell pepper
1	cup dry white wine
1	large garlic clove, minced
1	(14-ounce) can diced tomatoes
1/2	cup beef broth
2	teaspoons chopped fresh rosemary
1	bay leaf
	Fresh rosemary sprigs (optional)

Preheat the oven to 350 degrees. Combine the flour, pepper and salt in a sealable plastic bag or shallow dish. Add the veal a few pieces at a time and coat well. Heat the olive oil in a Dutch oven or large ovenproof skillet over medium-high heat. Add the veal and brown on all sides. Remove the veal from the pan. Reduce the heat to medium and add the carrots, celery, onion, bell pepper, wine and garlic. Cook for 5 minutes, stirring to deglaze the pan. Return the veal to the pan and add the undrained tomatoes, beef broth, rosemary and bay leaf. Bake, covered, for 2 hours or until the veal is tender. Discard the bay leaf. Spoon the sauce from the pan over the veal to serve. Garnish with fresh rosemary, if desired.

Serves 4 to 6

Veal and Mushroom Piccata

2   pounds veal cutlets, cut into
      1$1/2$-inch strips
      All-purpose flour
      Salt and pepper to taste
2   tablespoons butter
1   tablespoon olive oil
$1/3$ cup dry white wine
$1/4$ cup ($1/2$ stick) butter
1   tablespoon lemon juice
1   pound mushrooms, sliced
      Chopped fresh parsley
      Hot cooked egg noodles

Place the veal between 2 pieces of plastic wrap and pound gently with a wooden mallet. Combine the flour, salt and pepper in a large sealable plastic bag. Add the veal a few pieces at a time and shake to coat well. Heat 2 tablespoons butter and the olive oil in a large skillet or saucepan over medium heat. Add the veal and sauté until lightly browned. Remove the veal and keep warm. Stir in the wine, 1/4 cup butter and the lemon juice and bring to a boil. Add the mushrooms and sauté until tender. Sprinkle with the parsley. To serve, spoon the mushrooms over the veal and noodles.

Serves 6 to 8

Sesame Lamb Chops

10	(1-inch-thick) rib or loin lamb chops
	Peanut oil
1/4	cup toasted sesame seeds
1/4	cup Dijon mustard
1/4	cup hoisin sauce
3	tablespoons sesame oil
3	tablespoons light brown sugar
2	tablespoons soy sauce
2	tablespoons minced garlic
2	teaspoons salt
2	teaspoons pepper
6	tablespoons rubbed sage

Preheat the oven to 450 degrees. Brown the lamb chops on both sides in a thin layer of the peanut oil in a large skillet over medium-high heat. Remove the chops and cool to room temperature. Combine the sesame seeds, Dijon mustard, hoisin sauce, sesame oil, brown sugar, soy sauce, garlic, salt and pepper in a large sealable plastic bag or a medium bowl and mix well. Add the chops 1 at a time and coat well on both sides. Place the chops in a large roasting pan. Stir a small amount of water into the sage in a small bowl. Sprinkle the sage mixture over the chops. Cover the pan with foil and place in the oven. Reduce the oven temperature to 400 degrees. Roast for 20 to 30 minutes. Remove from the oven and serve.

Serves 5

The photograph for this recipe appears on page 78.

Oven-Barbecued Pork

1   (5-pound) bone-in Boston butt pork shoulder roast, trimmed

1/4 cup Dry Barbecue Rub (at right)

3   cups Old-Fashioned Barbecue Sauce (page 90)

Preheat the oven to 250 degrees. Line a roasting pan with heavy-duty foil and place the roast in the pan. Sprinkle the Dry Barbecue Rub evenly over the entire surface of the roast. Cover the pan with a tent of foil, folding the edges over the pan to seal. Roast for 8 to 9 hours or until the meat falls off the bone when pierced with a fork. Let cool. Shred the meat using 2 forks. Discard any fat. Heat the Old-Fashioned Barbecue Sauce and mix into the shredded pork.

Serves 12

Dry Barbecue Rub

1/2 cup paprika

6   tablespoons granulated sugar

1/4 cup chili powder

1/4 cup ground cumin

1/4 cup black pepper

1/4 cup salt

2   tablespoons brown sugar

1   teaspoon cayenne pepper

Combine the paprika, granulated sugar, chili powder, cumin, black pepper, salt, brown sugar and cayenne pepper in a small bowl and mix well. Store in an airtight container in a cool dry place. Use to coat pork, chicken or ribs for roasting or grilling.

Makes about 2 cups

OLD-FASHIONED BARBECUE SAUCE

1/2 cup (1 stick) butter
1   cup vinegar
1   tablespoon ketchup
1   teaspoon black pepper
1   teaspoon red pepper flakes
1   teaspoon salt
1   teaspoon Tabasco sauce
1   teaspoon prepared mustard

Melt the butter in a small saucepan. Add the vinegar, ketchup, black pepper, red pepper flakes, salt, Tabasco sauce and mustard and mix well. Simmer to blend the flavors. Use to baste chicken or pork during grilling.

Makes about 1 1/2 cups

Evelyn Wood, President 1980–1981

GRILLED PORK TENDERLOINS

1/2 cup teriyaki sauce
1/2 cup soy sauce
3   tablespoons brown sugar
1   tablespoon sesame seeds
1   tablespoon vegetable oil
2   green onions, chopped
1   garlic clove, pressed
1/2 teaspoon ground ginger
1/2 teaspoon pepper
3   (1 1/2-pound) packages
     pork tenderloins

Combine all the ingredients except the pork tenderloins in a large sealable plastic bag or a shallow dish. Add the pork tenderloins, turning to coat evenly. Marinate, covered, in the refrigerator for 3 hours. Preheat the grill to 350 degrees and place the tenderloins on a grill rack coated with nonstick cooking spray. Grill, covered, directly over medium-hot coals for 15 to 20 minutes or until a meat thermometer inserted in the center registers 160 degrees, turning once with tongs. Remove the meat to a clean baking dish or cutting board and let stand, loosely covered with foil, for 5 minutes. Slice to serve.

Serves 12 to 15

Cindy Armfield, President 2002–2003

Honey Sesame Pork Tenderloin

1/2   cup soy sauce
2   garlic cloves, minced
1   tablespoon grated fresh ginger
1   tablespoon sesame oil
1   to 1 1/2 pounds pork tenderloin
1/4   cup honey
2   tablespoons dark brown sugar
1/4   cup sesame seeds

Combine the soy sauce, garlic, ginger and sesame oil in a large sealable plastic bag. Add the tenderloin, turning to coat evenly. Marinate, covered, in the refrigerator for 2 hours or longer. Preheat the oven to 375 degrees. Combine the honey and brown sugar in a shallow dish. Remove the tenderloin from the marinade and pat dry with a paper towel. Discard the marinade. Roll the tenderloin in the honey mixture, then in the sesame seeds to coat. Place in a shallow roasting pan. Roast for 20 to 30 minutes or until a meat thermometer inserted in the center registers 160 degrees. Remove the meat to a cutting board and let stand, loosely covered with foil, for 5 minutes. Slice to serve.

Serves 4 to 6

CURRY-CRANBERRY PORK CHOPS

2	teaspoons curry powder
1/4	teaspoon ground ginger
6	pork chops
	All-purpose flour
1	tablespoon shortening
1	(16-ounce) can whole cranberry sauce
1/4	cup dry white wine
1/2	teaspoon salt
1/2	teaspoon pepper
1/2	teaspoon grated lemon zest

Preheat the oven to 350 degrees. Combine the curry powder and ginger and rub over both sides of the pork chops. Coat the chops with flour. Heat the shortening in a large skillet. Add the chops and brown on both sides. Remove the chops to a shallow baking dish. Drain the fat from the skillet and add the cranberry sauce, wine, salt, pepper and lemon zest. Bring to a boil, stirring constantly. Pour over the chops. Bake, uncovered, for 45 minutes or until the chops are tender.

Serves 6

Pattie Betts, President 1954–1955

Sweet-and-Sour Slow-Cooker Spareribs

3   to 4 pounds pork spareribs
     Salt and pepper to taste
1   cup low-sodium chicken broth
1/4   cup packed brown sugar, or to taste
1/4   cup apple cider vinegar
1   tablespoon soy sauce
1   onion, thinly sliced
2   tablespoons cornstarch
1   (11-ounce) can mandarin
     oranges, drained
     Hot cooked rice or noodles

Preheat the oven to 400 degrees. Cut the spareribs into serving-size pieces and season with salt and pepper. Place on a rack in a shallow baking pan or on a broiler pan and roast for 15 minutes. Turn the ribs and roast for 10 to 15 minutes longer or until browned; drain. Place the ribs in a slow cooker. Combine the chicken broth, brown sugar, vinegar and soy sauce in a bowl and mix well. Pour over the ribs. Cook, covered, on Low for 6 to 8 hours. Turn the slow cooker to High and add the onion. Combine the cornstarch and a small amount of cold water in a small bowl, stirring until dissolved. Stir into the rib mixture. Cook, covered, for 10 to 15 minutes or until slightly thickened. Stir in the oranges and cook, covered, for 5 minutes. Serve over rice or noodles.

Serves 4 to 6

NORTH CAROLINA BARBECUE PICNIC

SOUTHERN SWEETENED TEA

OVEN-BARBECUED PORK

OLD-FASHIONED BARBECUE SAUCE

SOUTHERN FRIED CHICKEN

BARBECUE SLAW

BLACK-EYED PEA SALAD

BETTY ANN'S BEANS

MACARONI AND CHEESE

CRISP SWEET PICKLES

BEST LEMON CAKE

BANANA PUDDING

Spaghetti alla Carbonara

4   garlic cloves, minced
2   tablespoons olive oil
1   tablespoon butter
1/2 pound pancetta or thick-sliced bacon,
     cut into pieces
1/4 cup dry white wine
16   ounces spaghetti
3   eggs
1/2 cup (2 ounces) grated Parmesan
     cheese
4   to 5 teaspoons grated Romano cheese
2   tablespoons chopped fresh parsley
     Freshly ground pepper to taste

Sauté the garlic in the olive oil and butter in a large skillet until golden brown. Add the pancetta and cook until crisp. Remove the pancetta mixture and reserve 2 tablespoons of the drippings in the skillet. Add the wine to the skillet and heat until it evaporates. Return the pancetta mixture to the skillet. Cook the spaghetti until al dente. Beat the eggs in a large serving bowl. Beat in the Parmesan cheese, Romano cheese, parsley and pepper. Drain the hot spaghetti and add to the egg mixture, tossing quickly to coat. Pour the pancetta mixture over the spaghetti and toss again. Serve immediately.

Serves 6 to 8

Quick Stromboli

1 loaf frozen bread dough, thawed, or
1 (13-ounce) package refrigerator
pizza dough
1/4 pound salami, sliced
4 ounces provolone cheese, sliced
1/4 pound shaved ham
4 ounces mozzarella cheese, shredded
1/4 pound bulk pork sausage, cooked and
crumbled
Melted butter
Grated Parmesan cheese
Italian seasoning
Garlic powder
Favorite marinara sauce

Let the bread dough rise and then roll it into a rectangle, or use the package directions for the pizza dough. Place the dough rectangle on a baking sheet. Preheat the oven to 350 degrees. Layer the salami, provolone cheese, ham, mozzarella cheese and sausage in the center of the dough. Fold the dough over and pinch the edges together to seal. Brush the top of the dough with melted butter. Sprinkle with Parmesan cheese, Italian seasoning and garlic powder. Prick the dough with a fork in several places. Bake for 30 minutes. Cool for 5 minutes before slicing. Serve with marinara sauce.

Serves 6

Beer Can Chicken

1	tablespoon brown sugar
1	tablespoon sweet paprika
2	teaspoons freshly ground black pepper
1	teaspoon chili powder
1/2	teaspoon garlic powder
1/2	teaspoon onion powder
	Cayenne pepper to taste
1	(3- to 4-pound) chicken
1	(12-ounce) can beer

Combine the brown sugar, paprika, black pepper, chili powder, garlic powder, onion powder and cayenne pepper in a small bowl and mix well. Loosen the chicken skin around the breast and thigh with your fingers. Rub a pinch of the spice mixture under the skin and into the chicken cavities. Sprinkle the remaining spice mixture over the chicken. Place the chicken in a large sealable plastic bag or cover with plastic wrap and place in a shallow dish. Marinate in the refrigerator for 1 to 6 hours. Preheat the oven to 350 degrees and place the oven rack in the lowest position. Open the beer can and remove about half the beer. Use an ice pick to poke 2 holes in the top of the beer can. Place the can in the center of a broiler pan lined with heavy-duty foil and arrange the chicken over the can with the legs and can forming a tripod. Bake for 1 1/2 to 2 hours or until the juices run clear when the thigh is pierced with a fork. Remove the chicken and can carefully to a serving platter, keeping the can upright. Let stand for 5 minutes. Carefully remove the can before serving the chicken.

Serves 4 to 6

Tip: *The chicken can also be cooked on a covered grill using indirect heat.*

Too-Busy-to-Cook Chicken

1   (6-ounce) package stove-top
      stuffing mix
1 1/4 cups water
1   Granny Smith apple, diced
1/4   cup vermouth
1   (3- to 4-pound) chicken
      Salt and pepper to taste
      Basil and tarragon (optional)
3   or 4 potatoes, quartered
1/2   cup baby carrots
4   or 5 ribs celery, cut into chunks
1   cup vermouth

Prepare the stuffing mix with 1 1/4 cups water using the package directions and adding the apple; cool. Stir in 1/4 cup vermouth. Season the chicken with salt, pepper, basil and tarragon. Stuff the chicken cavities with the prepared stuffing. Place the potatoes and carrots on the bottom of a slow cooker and top with the chicken. Arrange the celery around the chicken. Pour 1 cup vermouth over the chicken. Cook, covered, on Low for 6 to 8 hours.

Serves 4 to 6

Parmesan Chicken

6   boneless skinless chicken breasts
6   tablespoons margarine, melted
3/4   cup bread crumbs
1/3   cup grated Parmesan cheese
1 1/2 tablespoons garlic salt

Preheat the oven to 325 degrees. Coat the chicken breasts with the margarine. Combine the bread crumbs, Parmesan cheese and garlic salt in a shallow dish and mix well. Roll the chicken in the bread crumb mixture, coating well. Place aluminum foil over the bottom of a baking dish. Arrange the chicken in the prepared dish. Bake, uncovered, for 45 minutes or until cooked through.

Serves 6

CHICKEN TARRAGON

3	tablespoons (or more) unsalted butter
2	tablespoons (or more) olive oil
6	boneless skinless chicken breasts
2	shallots, thinly sliced
1	cup chicken stock
1/2	cup dry white wine
2	garlic cloves, minced
3/4	cup heavy cream or whipping cream
3	tablespoons grainy Dijon mustard
1	tablespoon chopped fresh tarragon, or 1 teaspoon dried tarragon
1	teaspoon fresh thyme leaves, or 1/2 teaspoon dried thyme
1/2	teaspoon salt
	Pinch of pepper

Heat the butter and olive oil in a large skillet over medium heat. Add the chicken and sauté on both sides until cooked through and lightly browned, adding more butter and olive oil as needed. Remove the chicken and keep warm. Add the shallots and sauté for 2 minutes. Stir in the chicken stock, wine and garlic and bring to a boil over medium-high heat. Reduce the heat and simmer until the liquid is reduced to 1/2 cup. Whisk in the cream, then the mustard, tarragon, thyme, salt and pepper. Return the chicken to the skillet and cook for about 5 minutes or until the chicken is heated through.

Serves 4 to 6

BAKED CHICKEN

Chicken pieces, as many as needed
Salt and pepper
All-purpose flour
Butter
Milk

Preheat the oven to 350 degrees. Arrange the chicken pieces in a greased baking dish and season with salt and pepper. Sprinkle with flour. Dot with butter. Pour enough milk around the chicken to cover the bottom of the dish. If more than 1 layer of chicken is needed, repeat the seasoning, addition of flour and butter for each layer. Bake, covered, for 1 hour or until cooked through.

Serves a variable amount

Nell H. Tucker, President 1948–1949

SOUTHERN FRIED CHICKEN

1   (3- to 4-pound) chicken, cut up
1   teaspoon salt
1   teaspoon pepper
2   cups buttermilk
    Self-rising flour
    Vegetable oil for frying

Season the chicken with the salt and pepper and place in a large sealable plastic bag. Add the buttermilk. Marinate in the refrigerator for 2 hours. Remove the chicken from the marinade; discard the marinade. Coat the chicken with flour. Heat 1 1/2 inches of oil to 360 degrees in a Dutch oven or deep heavy skillet. Add the chicken a few pieces at a time. Cook, covered, for 6 minutes. Cook, uncovered, for an additional 8 minutes. Turn the chicken over and cook, covered, for 6 minutes. Cook, uncovered, for an additional 6 to 8 minutes or until golden brown. Watch carefully during the last few minutes of cooking, turning if needed to prevent overbrowning. Drain on paper towels. Repeat the cooking process with the remaining chicken.

Serves 4 to 6

THREE-IN-ONE CASSEROLE

6 boneless skinless chicken breasts

1 (10-ounce) can chicken broth

1/2 cup dry white wine

2 (15-ounce) cans French-style green beans, drained

1/2 (14-ounce) package quick-cooking rice

1 (10-ounce) can cream of mushroom soup

1 (10-ounce) can cream of chicken soup

1/4 to 1/2 cup mayonnaise

1 teaspoon Tabasco sauce

1/4 cup dry white wine

Preheat the oven to 325 degrees. Cook the chicken in the chicken broth and 1/2 cup wine in a large saucepan until tender. Remove the chicken, reserving the broth in the pan. Add the beans to the reserved broth and heat through. Remove the beans from the pan, reserving the broth. Add the rice to the broth and cook using the package directions. Layer the beans, rice and chicken in a greased baking dish. Stir together the soups, mayonnaise, Tabasco sauce and 1/4 cup wine in a bowl. Pour over the chicken. Bake until hot and bubbly.

Serves 6

Chicken with Artichokes and Mushrooms

3/4 cup uncooked rice
2 cups sliced mushrooms
1/2 cup chopped onion
2 tablespoons butter
1 (10-ounce) can cream of
  mushroom soup
1/2 cup mayonnaise
1/2 cup sour cream, at room temperature
1/2 cup dry sherry or white wine
1 (8-ounce) can sliced water
  chestnuts, drained
  Salt and pepper to taste
1 (14-ounce) can artichoke hearts,
  drained and quartered
2 cups chopped cooked chicken breasts
1 cup (4 ounces) shredded sharp
  Cheddar cheese

Preheat the oven to 350 degrees. Cook the rice using the package directions. Sauté the mushrooms and onion in the butter in a large skillet. Combine the soup, mayonnaise, sour cream, sherry, water chestnuts, salt and pepper in a bowl and mix well. Stir into the mushrooms. Layer the artichokes in a buttered 9×13-inch baking dish. Top evenly with the rice and chicken. Pour the mushroom mixture over the chicken. Sprinkle with the cheese. Bake for 25 to 30 minutes.

Serves 6 to 8

Mary Louise Stone, President 1965–1966

Chicken Fajita Pizza

1   (13-ounce) package refrigerator pizza
    crust, or 1 large prepared refrigerator
    pizza crust
2   large chicken breasts, skinned, boned
    and cut into strips (about 2 cups)
1   tablespoon canola oil
2   teaspoons chili powder
1   teaspoon salt
1/2 teaspoon garlic powder
1   small sweet onion, sliced
1   small green bell pepper, chopped
1   cup salsa
8   ounces Monterey Jack cheese, shredded
    Chopped tomatoes, shredded lettuce
    and/or sour cream

Preheat the oven to 425 degrees. Place
the pizza crust on a lightly greased baking
sheet. Sauté the chicken in the canola oil in
a large skillet over medium-high heat for
5 minutes or until tender. Stir in the chili
powder, salt and garlic powder. Remove the
chicken mixture from the skillet. Add the
onion and bell pepper to the skillet and
sauté for 5 minutes or until tender. Spread
the salsa on the pizza crust. Top with the
chicken, onion mixture and cheese. Bake
for 10 to 12 minutes or until the cheese
is melted. Serve with desired toppings.

Serves 4 to 6

CHICKEN PIE

1/4	cup (1/2 stick) butter
1/4	cup all-purpose flour
1	teaspoon salt
1/4	teaspoon pepper
2	cups chicken stock
2/3	cup cream or milk
2	cups chopped cooked chicken
1	cup cooked carrots
1	cup cooked peas
	Dash of hot red pepper sauce
1	refrigerator pie pastry

Preheat the oven to 425 degrees. Melt the butter in a large saucepan. Remove from the heat and stir in the flour, salt and pepper until smooth. Stir in the chicken stock and cream. Bring to a boil, stirring constantly. Cook until thickened, stirring constantly. Add the chicken, carrots, peas and hot sauce. Heat through. Pour into a 9-inch round baking dish and top with the pie pastry. Seal the edge of the pastry to the dish; flute, if desired. Cut small slits in the pastry to vent. Bake for 20 to 25 minutes or until the crust is golden brown. Cool for 5 minutes before serving.

Serves 4

Founded in 1904, Adams Millis initially produced twenty thousand dozen pairs of black socks annually. In 1989, the company had grown to produce over twenty million dozen pairs of socks annually and was purchased that same year by the Sara Lee Corporation.

Sweet-and-Tangy Chicken

6   chicken breasts
1   (8-ounce) bottle Russian
     salad dressing
1   envelope onion soup mix
1   (10- to 12-ounce) jar apricot preserves

Preheat the oven to 350 degrees. Place the chicken in a single layer in a greased 9×13-inch or other shallow baking dish. Combine the salad dressing, soup mix and preserves in a bowl and mix well. Pour over the chicken. Bake, uncovered, for 1 hour or until the chicken is cooked through.

Serves 6

Hot Chicken Salad

2   cups chopped cooked chicken
3   hard-cooked eggs, chopped
1   cup chopped celery
1/2 cup slivered almonds
1/4 cup mayonnaise
1   tablespoon lemon juice
1   (10-ounce) can cream of chicken soup
     Salt and pepper to taste
     Crushed potato chips

Preheat the oven to 400 degrees. Mix the chicken, eggs, celery, almonds, mayonnaise, lemon juice, soup, salt and pepper in a large bowl. Spread evenly in a 9×13-inch baking dish. Bake for 10 minutes. Top with the crushed potato chips. Return to the oven and bake for 10 minutes longer or until hot and bubbly.

Serves 6

Bow Tie Pesto Chicken

2 1/2 cups chopped cooked chicken
2   (10-ounce) cans cream of
    chicken soup
16 ounces bow tie pasta, cooked
    and drained
1   (12-ounce) jar marinated artichoke
    hearts, drained and chopped
1   cup oil-packed sun-dried tomatoes,
    cut into strips
3/4 cup (3 ounces) freshly grated
    Parmesan cheese
1   (7-ounce) container pesto
1   (4-ounce) jar diced pimentos
1/4 cup (1 ounce) freshly grated
    Parmesan cheese

Preheat the oven to 350 degrees. Combine
the chicken, soup, pasta, artichokes,
sun-dried tomatoes, 3/4 cup Parmesan
cheese, the pesto and pimentos in a large
bowl and mix well. Spoon into a greased
3 1/2-quart baking dish. Sprinkle with
1/4 cup Parmesan cheese. Bake, covered,
for 15 minutes. Bake, uncovered, for 20 to
25 minutes longer or until hot and bubbly.

Serves 6 to 8

Easy Chicken Tetrazzini

1   (8-ounce) can sliced mushrooms
2   tablespoons butter
2   cups (or more) chopped cooked
    chicken
2   (10-ounce) cans cream of celery soup
1   cup sour cream, at room temperature
1   teaspoon salt
1/2 teaspoon pepper
16 ounces spaghetti, cooked and drained
    Grated Parmesan cheese

Preheat the oven to 350 degrees. Drain the
mushrooms, reserving the liquid. Sauté the
mushrooms in the butter in a large skillet.
Add the chicken, soup, sour cream, salt and
pepper and mix well. Add the reserved
liquid or chicken broth if the mixture is too
thick. Place a layer of spaghetti in a greased
9×13-inch baking dish and top with a layer
of the chicken mixture. Repeat the layers.
Sprinkle generously with Parmesan cheese.
Bake for 25 minutes or until hot and bubbly.

Serves 6 to 8

Ann Freeze, President 1960–1961

Chicken Lasagna

1   (10-ounce) can cream of
    mushroom soup
2/3 cup milk
1   teaspoon salt
1/2 teaspoon poultry seasoning
8   ounces cream cheese, softened
16 ounces cottage cheese
1/3 cup minced onion
1/3 cup chopped green bell pepper
1/3 cup sliced pimento-stuffed olives
1   teaspoon chopped parsley
8   ounces (12 strips) wide lasagna
    noodles, cooked and drained
2   (2-pound) chickens, cooked, boned
    and chopped
1   cup buttered bread crumbs

Preheat the oven to 325 degrees. Combine the soup, milk, salt and poultry seasoning in a large saucepan and heat through. Add the cream cheese and cottage cheese and mix well. Combine the onion, bell pepper, olives and parsley in a bowl and mix well. Layer the noodles, cheese mixture, onion mixture and chicken in a greased 9×13-inch or larger shallow baking dish. Repeat the layers of noodles, cheese mixture, onion mixture and chicken until all the ingredients are used. Top with the bread crumbs. Bake for 30 minutes or until hot and bubbly. Let stand for 5 minutes before serving.

Serves 8 to 10

Wellington Cornish Hens

6   (1-pound) frozen Rock Cornish game
     hens, thawed
1 1/2 teaspoons salt
     Pepper
3   egg whites
1   (6-ounce) package long grain and wild
     rice mix
1/4 cup grated orange zest
3   (8-ounce) packages refrigerator
     crescent rolls
3   egg yolks, beaten
2   (10-ounce) jars red currant jelly
1   tablespoon prepared mustard
1   tablespoon port
1/4 cup fresh lemon juice
1   (1-pound) jar spiced whole crab
     apples, drained (optional)
1   bunch watercress (optional)

Pat the game hens dry and tie the legs together with cooking twine. Season each game hen with 1/4 teaspoon salt and a dash of pepper and brush with unbeaten egg white. Place the game hens in a large shallow baking dish and refrigerate.

Cook the rice using the package directions for drier rice. Stir in the orange zest. Spoon the rice into the game hen cavities and refrigerate.

Open 1 package of the crescent rolls and unroll half the dough on a floured surface. Press the perforated edges of 2 triangles together to form a square. Roll out to an 8-inch circle with a floured rolling pin.

Remove 1 stuffed game hen from the refrigerator and place it breast side up on a wooden board. Place the dough circle over the game hen and press the dough over the body, tucking under to seal. Brush the dough with some of the egg yolks. Place the game hen on a large baking sheet.

Preheat the oven to 375 degrees. Repeat the process of rolling out the dough, covering each game hen with dough and brushing with egg yolk. Bake for 1 hour or until a meat fork can be easily inserted in the thigh.

Heat the jelly in a saucepan until melted. Stir in the mustard, wine and lemon juice until blended. Keep warm over low heat. Arrange the game hens on a heated platter and garnish with the crab apples and watercress. Serve with the currant sauce.

Serves 6

Betsy Hutchens, President 1975–1976

Grits and Grunts

1	pound farm-raised catfish fillets or other flaky white fish
1/4	cup cornmeal
1/4	cup bread crumbs
1/2	teaspoon salt
1/2	teaspoon paprika
1/4	teaspoon dill weed
1/8	teaspoon pepper
3/4	cup milk
3	tablespoons butter, melted
	Hot cooked grits

Preheat the oven to 450 degrees. Cut the fish into 1-inch strips. Combine the cornmeal, bread crumbs, salt, paprika, dill weed and pepper in a shallow dish and mix well. Combine the milk and butter in a bowl. Dip the fish a few strips at a time into the milk mixture. Coat with the cornmeal mixture. Place the fish on a well-greased rimmed baking sheet. Bake for 10 minutes. Serve with the grits.

Serves 4

Drunken Crawfish Pie

1/2	cup (1 stick) butter
1/4	cup all-purpose flour
1	cup chopped onion
1/2	cup chopped green onions
1/3	cup chopped green bell pepper
3	tablespoons chopped celery
3	tablespoons minced fresh parsley
2	teaspoons minced garlic
1/4	cup heavy cream or whipping cream
3	tablespoons brandy
1	teaspoon salt
3/4	teaspoon pepper
2	pounds crawfish tail meat
1	unbaked (9-inch) pie shell

Preheat the oven to 350 degrees. Melt the butter in a large saucepan. Add the flour gradually, stirring constantly until smooth. Add the onion, green onions, bell pepper, celery, parsley and garlic and cook until tender. Add the cream, brandy, salt and pepper. Cook over low heat for 3 minutes, stirring constantly. Stir in the crawfish. Remove from the heat and cool slightly. Spoon the crawfish mixture into the pie shell. Bake for 25 to 30 minutes.

Serves 6

Crab Cakes with Caper Sauce

CRAB CAKES

1	egg
1	teaspoon honey mustard or Dijon mustard
1	tablespoon light mayonnaise
1/2	teaspoon Old Bay seasoning
1/2	teaspoon chopped parsley
1/3	pound lump crab meat, shells removed
	Herb-seasoned stuffing mix
	Olive oil and butter for sautéing

CAPER SAUCE

2	tablespoons mayonnaise
	Dijon mustard to taste
	Capers to taste

For the crab cakes, beat the egg in a medium bowl. Add the honey mustard, mayonnaise, Old Bay seasoning and parsley and mix well. Stir in the crab meat and enough stuffing mix to hold the mixture together. Shape into 2 cakes. Chill, covered, for 2 hours or longer. Sauté the crab cakes in the olive oil and butter in a skillet until golden brown on both sides.

For the sauce, mix the mayonnaise, Dijon mustard and capers in a small bowl. Chill until ready to serve.

Serves 2

BAKED CRAB MEAT WITH SHERRY

1/2 cup dry sherry
1 pound crab meat, shells removed
3 or 4 slices soft bread, torn into pieces
1/4 cup (1/2 stick) butter, melted
1/2 cup light cream
1/2 cup mayonnaise
Juice of 1/2 lemon
Salt and pepper to taste
1/2 cup (2 ounces) grated
Parmesan cheese
Buttered bread crumbs

Pour the sherry over the crab meat in a large bowl. Marinate, covered, in the refrigerator for several hours. Drain the crab meat and discard the marinade. Preheat the oven to 350 degrees. Place the bread in a medium bowl. Add the butter, cream, mayonnaise, lemon juice, salt and pepper and mix well. Add the bread mixture to the crab meat and mix gently. Spoon the crab mixture into buttered individual baking shells or a 2-quart baking dish. Top with the cheese and bread crumbs. Bake for 20 to 30 minutes or until hot and bubbly.

Serves 4

Betsy Hoak, President 1967–1968

Tip: *This dish can be made ahead, baked, and frozen. Reheat to serve.*

LOBSTER CHEESECAKE

24   ounces cream cheese, softened

3   eggs, at room temperature

1   cup sour cream, at room temperature

2   tablespoons chopped fresh dill weed

2   tablespoons lemon juice

1   tablespoon fish bouillon

1 1/2 cups finely chopped cooked lobster meat

3   tablespoons all-purpose flour

1   tablespoon butter or margarine, softened

1/2 cup crushed unsalted pretzels
     Fresh dill weed (optional)

Preheat the oven to 350 degrees. Beat the cream cheese in a large mixing bowl until light and fluffy. Beat in the eggs 1 at a time. Stir in the sour cream, dill weed, lemon juice and bouillon. Place the lobster and flour in a large sealable plastic bag and shake to coat. Add the lobster to the cream cheese mixture and mix well. Coat the bottom of a 9-inch springform pan with the butter and coat evenly with the crushed pretzels. Pour the lobster mixture over the pretzels and place the pan on a baking sheet. Bake for 55 to 75 minutes or until the center is set. Turn off the heat and leave the cheesecake in the oven for 1 hour or longer with the oven door ajar. Remove to a wire rack to cool completely. Chill in the pan overnight. Place on a serving plate and remove the side of the pan. Garnish with fresh dill weed.

Serves 8

SCALLOPED OYSTERS

1	sleeve Ritz crackers, crushed
1/4	cup (1/2 stick) margarine
2	pints fresh oysters, lightly drained
2	tablespoons finely chopped onion
1	teaspoon celery seeds, or 2 tablespoons finely chopped celery (optional)
	Lemon pepper
1	sleeve Ritz crackers, crushed
1/4	cup (1/2 stick) margarine

Preheat the oven to 350 degrees. Brown 1 sleeve of crushed crackers in 1/4 cup margarine in a large skillet over medium heat, stirring constantly. Place in a 7×11-inch or other shallow baking dish. Arrange the oysters over the crackers. Top evenly with the onion, celery seeds and lemon pepper. Brown 1 sleeve of crushed crackers in 1/4 cup margarine in the skillet over medium heat, stirring constantly. Sprinkle over the oysters. Bake for 30 minutes or until hot and bubbly.

Serves 8

BRUNSWICK SCALLOPS WITH GIN

3/4	cup all-purpose flour
1	pound scallops, rinsed
1/4	cup (1/2 stick) butter
1	tablespoon vegetable oil
3/4	cup gin
1	cup light cream
1 1/2	tablespoons lemon juice
	Salt and pepper to taste
	Chopped fresh parsley and tarragon
	Hot cooked rice

Place the flour in a sealable plastic bag or paper bag and add the scallops. Shake to coat well. Heat the butter and oil in a large skillet and add the scallops in a single layer. Sauté until lightly browned on both sides. Stir in the gin, cream, lemon juice, salt and pepper. Simmer, covered, for 2 to 4 minutes or until the scallops are opaque. Sprinkle with parsley and tarragon and serve over rice.

Serves 4

Greek Shrimp over Pasta

2   garlic cloves, chopped
2   tablespoons olive oil
1   (28-ounce) can diced tomatoes
1/2   cup dry white wine
2   teaspoons basil
2   teaspoons oregano
    Salt and pepper to taste
16   ounces linguini
1   pound shrimp, peeled and deveined
8   ounces feta cheese, crumbled

Sauté the garlic in the olive oil in a large skillet. Add the tomatoes, wine, basil, oregano, salt and pepper and simmer for about 20 minutes. Cook the linguini using the package directions; drain. Add the shrimp and feta cheese to the tomato mixture. Cook for 5 to 10 minutes or until the shrimp turn pink. Serve the shrimp over the hot linguini. Serve with a fresh green salad and crusty French bread.

Serves 4 to 6

Judy Walker, President 1979–1980

Shrimp Newburg

2   tablespoons butter
2   to 3 tablespoons all-purpose flour
1   cup cream or milk
3   tablespoons ketchup
3/4   tablespoon Worcestershire sauce
1   pound shrimp, peeled, deveined and cooked
    Salt, paprika and cayenne pepper to taste
    Hot cooked grits pressed into a ring mold or hot cooked rice

Melt the butter in a large skillet and stir in the flour until smooth. Stir in the cream until blended. Cook until thickened, stirring constantly. Stir in the ketchup and Worcestershire sauce. Add the shrimp and heat through. Season with the salt, paprika and cayenne pepper. Serve the shrimp in a grits ring or over rice.

Serves 4

Orzo with Shrimp

1/2 cup shredded carrots
1/2 cup chopped green bell pepper
1/2 cup chopped onion
    Olive oil
3 cups vegetable broth or chicken broth
1 1/4 cups orzo
1/2 cup green peas (optional)
1/2 cup medium shrimp, peeled
    Chopped garlic to taste
1 Roma tomato, finely chopped
1/2 cup chopped sun-dried tomatoes
    (optional)
    Garlic pepper to taste
1/4 cup (1 ounce) grated Parmesan cheese
    Additional grated Parmesan cheese

Sauté the carrots, bell pepper and onion in olive oil in a skillet until the onion is translucent. Bring the vegetable broth to a boil in a large saucepan. Add the orzo, sautéed vegetables and peas and simmer for 5 minutes. Sauté the shrimp and garlic in the skillet briefly. Add the Roma tomato, sun-dried tomatoes and garlic pepper to the orzo mixture. Cook, covered, until all the liquid is absorbed. Stir in the shrimp mixture and 1/4 cup Parmesan cheese and let stand, covered, for 2 minutes. Serve with additional Parmesan cheese.

Serves 4

Courtney Best, President 1985–1986

Shrimp and Grits

1   onion, chopped
2   tablespoons bacon drippings
1 1/2 tablespoons all-purpose flour
1 1/2 cups shrimp, peeled and deveined
1 1/2 cups water
2   tablespoons ketchup
1   teaspoon Worcestershire sauce
4   drops of hot red pepper sauce
     Salt and pepper to taste
3   cups hot cooked grits

Sauté the onion in the bacon drippings in a large skillet. Stir in the flour. Cook until browned, stirring constantly. Add the shrimp, water, ketchup, Worcestershire sauce, hot sauce, salt and pepper. Simmer for 15 to 20 minutes, stirring occasionally and adding additional water if needed. Serve over the grits.

Serves 4 to 6

Hatteras Yachts, founded by textile executive Willis Slane, had production facilities in High Point and New Bern, North Carolina. During the late twentieth century, the company dominated as the world's leading maker of luxury yachts.

Lemon Fettuccini with Asparagus

8   ounces fettuccini

1/2   pound fresh asparagus, cut into
      1-inch pieces
      Salt to taste

2   tablespoons butter, melted

2   egg yolks

1   cup heavy cream or whipping cream

1/2   cup (2 ounces) freshly grated
      Parmesan cheese

1   tablespoon chopped chives

1   teaspoon grated lemon zest
      Freshly ground pepper to taste

2   slices lemon, halved

Cook the fettuccini using the package directions; drain. Cook the asparagus in boiling salted water in a saucepan for 3 minutes or until tender; drain and add to the fettuccini. Add the butter and toss gently. Whisk the egg yolks in a small bowl. Whisk in the cream and cheese. Pour the cream mixture into a large saucepan and cook over medium-low heat for 3 to 4 minutes or until the cheese is melted, stirring constantly. Stir in the chives, lemon zest, salt and pepper. Add the fettuccini mixture to the pan and toss well to coat with the sauce. Serve immediately. Garnish each serving with a half slice of lemon.

Serves 4

Lasagna Swirls

2   (10-ounce) packages frozen chopped spinach, thawed and drained

16   ounces ricotta cheese

2   cups (8 ounces) shredded mozzarella cheese

1   cup (4 ounces) grated Parmesan cheese

8   ounces cream cheese, softened

1/2 teaspoon basil

1/4 teaspoon oregano

1/4 teaspoon salt

1/4 teaspoon pepper

8   ounces lasagna noodles, cooked and drained

1   (15-ounce) can tomato sauce

1/2 cup (2 ounces) grated Parmesan cheese

Preheat the oven to 350 degrees. Combine the spinach, ricotta cheese, mozzarella cheese, 1 cup Parmesan cheese, the cream cheese, basil, oregano, salt and pepper in a large bowl and mix well. Spread about 1/2 cup of the spinach mixture on each lasagna noodle and roll to enclose the filling, starting at 1 of the short sides. Place the lasagna rolls seam side down in a greased 9×13-inch baking dish. Pour the tomato sauce evenly over the rolls and sprinkle with 1/2 cup Parmesan cheese. Bake for 35 minutes.

Serves 5

COMPLEMENTS

VEGETABLES

&

SIDE DISHES

Asparagus Casserole

1   (10-ounce) can cream of
     mushroom soup
3   tablespoons (or more) milk
1   (15-ounce) can asparagus, drained
1   (16-ounce) can English peas, drained
2   hard-cooked eggs, chopped
     Chopped almonds or crushed
     cheese crackers

Preheat the oven to 325 degrees. Combine the soup and milk in a bowl and stir until the mixture is of a thick sauce consistency, adding additional milk if necessary. Add the asparagus and peas and mix well. Spoon the mixture into a baking dish. Top with the eggs and sprinkle with almonds or cheese crackers. Bake for 30 to 35 minutes or until bubbly.

Serves 6

Betty Ann's Beans

1/2 pound bacon
1   large onion, chopped
1   (16-ounce) can baked beans, without
     tomato sauce
1   (16-ounce) can kidney beans, drained
1   (9-ounce) can lima beans, drained
1/2 cup ketchup
1/2 cup water
2   tablespoons vinegar
1   tablespoon brown sugar
1   teaspoon dry mustard
     Salt and pepper to taste

Preheat the oven to 350 degrees. Fry the bacon in a skillet until crisp. Remove the bacon to a paper towel-lined plate, reserving a small amount of the drippings. Sauté the onion in the reserved drippings until soft. Crumble the bacon into a bowl. Add the onion, baked beans, kidney beans, lima beans, ketchup, water, vinegar, brown sugar, mustard, salt and pepper and mix well. Spoon into a baking dish. Bake for 45 to 60 minutes or until hot and bubbly.

Serves 8 to 10

French Green Bean Casserole

1	small onion, finely chopped
1	(8-ounce) can mushrooms, drained
1/2	cup (1 stick) butter
2	cups warm milk
1/4	cup all-purpose flour
1	teaspoon Accent
1	teaspoon salt
1/4	teaspoon pepper
2	teaspoons soy sauce
1/8	teaspoon hot red pepper sauce
3	(10-ounce) packages frozen French-style green beans, cooked and drained
3/4	cup (3 ounces) shredded sharp Cheddar cheese
1	(8-ounce) can sliced water chestnuts, drained
	Slivered or sliced buttered almonds

Preheat the oven to 375 degrees. Sauté the onion and mushrooms in the butter in a skillet until the onion is tender. Combine the milk, flour, Accent, salt, pepper, soy sauce and hot sauce in a large bowl and mix well. Add the green beans and mix well. Stir in the onion mixture, cheese and water chestnuts. Spoon the mixture into a baking dish. Sprinkle with almonds. Bake for 30 minutes or until bubbly.

Serves 8 to 10

Wink Cottam, President 1962–1963

THREE-BEAN BAKE

4   slices bacon, chopped
1   onion, chopped
1   (16-ounce) can baked beans
1   (16-ounce) can kidney beans, drained
1   (15-ounce) can pinto beans, drained
4   ounces Cheddar cheese, cubed
1/2 cup packed brown sugar
1/3 cup ketchup
2   teaspoons Worcestershire sauce
     Grated Parmesan cheese

Preheat the oven to 350 degrees. Cook the bacon and onion in a skillet over medium heat until the bacon is lightly browned, stirring frequently; drain. Combine with the baked beans, kidney beans, pinto beans, Cheddar cheese, brown sugar, ketchup and Worcestershire sauce in a large bowl and mix well. Spoon into a buttered baking dish.

Bake for 30 to 40 minutes or until hot and bubbly. Sprinkle with Parmesan cheese. Bake for 5 minutes longer. Remove from the oven and let stand for 30 minutes or longer until thickened.

Serves 8 to 10

BROCCOLI CASSEROLE

2   (10-ounce) packages frozen chopped broccoli
2   eggs, beaten
1   (10-ounce) can cream of mushroom soup
1   cup (4 ounces) shredded sharp Cheddar cheese
1   cup mayonnaise
1   small onion, chopped
     Salt and pepper to taste
1   sleeve Ritz crackers, crushed
     Butter

Preheat the oven to 350 degrees. Cook the broccoli using the package directions for 5 minutes or until tender-crisp; drain. Combine the broccoli with the eggs, soup, cheese, mayonnaise, onion, salt and pepper in a large bowl and mix well. Spoon into a 2 1/2-quart baking dish. Sprinkle with the cracker crumbs. Dot with butter. Bake for 45 to 50 minutes or until hot and bubbly.

Serves 8

Wanna Blanton, President 1972–1973

Corn Pudding

2 cups fresh corn, partially drained
2 eggs, lightly beaten
2 cups scalded evaporated milk
1 1/2 tablespoons butter, melted
1/4 cup sugar
1 teaspoon salt
1/8 teaspoon pepper

Preheat the oven to 325 degrees. Combine the corn, eggs, evaporated milk, butter, sugar, salt and pepper in a bowl and mix gently. Spoon into a buttered baking dish. Bake for 1 hour.

Serves 4 to 6

Kendra Biddle, President 1995–1996

Sherry Portobello Mushrooms

1 small onion, finely chopped
3 tablespoons butter
1 pound portobello mushrooms, sliced
1/2 cup cooking sherry
2 tablespoons Worcestershire sauce
1/4 teaspoon sugar
1/8 teaspoon cinnamon
1/8 teaspoon nutmeg
1 cup sour cream, at room temperature
   Salt and pepper to taste
   Hot cooked rice

Sauté the onion in the butter in a skillet over medium heat until soft. Add the mushrooms and cook for 5 minutes on each side or just until tender. Add the sherry, Worcestershire sauce, sugar, cinnamon and nutmeg and cook until the liquid is reduced by 1/2, stirring frequently. Add the sour cream and simmer until the mixture is heated through, stirring frequently. Do not boil. Season with salt and pepper. Serve over rice.

Serves 4

Martha Mitchell Adams, President 1997–1998

Onion Pie

1	cup crushed Ritz crackers
2	tablespoons margarine, melted
2	cups thinly sliced onions
1	tablespoon olive oil
1	tablespoon water
2	eggs, beaten, or an equivalent amount of pasteurized egg substitute
3/4	cup milk
3/4	teaspoon salt
	Pepper to taste
1/2	cup (2 ounces) shredded sharp Cheddar cheese

Preheat the oven to 350 degrees. Combine the cracker crumbs and margarine in a bowl and mix well. Spread over the bottom of a 9-inch pie plate or 9-inch square baking dish. Combine the onions with the olive oil and water in a saucepan and cook over medium heat for 4 to 5 minutes or until soft. Spoon the onions over the cracker layer. Combine the eggs, milk, salt and pepper in a small bowl and mix well. Pour over the onions. Sprinkle with the cheese. Bake for 30 to 35 minutes or until hot and bubbly.

Serves 8

Lorraine Gayle, President 1955–1956

Onion Strudel

3	Vidalia onions, finely chopped
2	garlic cloves, finely chopped
2	tablespoons olive oil
2	teaspoons oregano
1	teaspoon marjoram
1	sheet frozen puff pastry, thawed
1	cup (4 ounces) shredded sharp Cheddar cheese, Swiss cheese or Gruyère cheese

Sauté the onions and garlic in the olive oil in a skillet over medium-low heat until tender and caramelized. Add the oregano and marjoram and cook for 1 to 2 minutes, stirring constantly.

Preheat the oven to 350 degrees. Unfold the pastry sheet onto a work surface and gently stretch it until slightly enlarged. Place on a baking sheet sprayed with nonstick cooking spray. Spoon the onion mixture down the center of the pastry sheet. Sprinkle with the cheese. Fold the pastry to enclose the filling. Bake for 15 to 20 minutes or until the pastry is puffed and golden brown. Cut into wedges and serve hot.

Serves 4 to 6

Tip: *To make individual puff pastries, cut a pastry sheet into circles or squares. Top with the onion mixture and cheese and place another pastry on the top, pressing the edges to seal. Bake using the above directions.*

Garlic Mashed Potatoes

2 pounds red potatoes, peeled
8 to 10 garlic cloves
1 3/4 cups heavy cream or whipping cream
1/2 cup (1 stick) unsalted butter
1 teaspoon salt
1/2 teaspoon freshly ground pepper

Combine the potatoes and garlic with water to cover in a large saucepan and bring to a boil. Boil until the potatoes are tender; drain. Heat the cream in a small saucepan over low heat. Combine the potatoes and garlic with the butter in a large bowl and beat with the whisk attachment of an electric mixer or mash with a potato masher. Add the cream gradually, beating constantly. Season with the salt and pepper and beat for 1 minute. Serve immediately.

Serves 8

The photograph for this recipe appears on page 120.

Baked Mashed Potatoes

8 to 10 boiling potatoes, peeled and chopped
  Salt and pepper to taste
8 ounces cream cheese, softened
2 eggs, beaten
1 tablespoon all-purpose flour
1 small onion, grated
2 tablespoons minced fresh parsley
2 tablespoons minced fresh chives
1 (4-ounce) can French-fried onions

Cook the potatoes in boiling water to cover in a large saucepan until tender; drain. Season with salt and pepper. Preheat the oven to 325 degrees. Beat the cream cheese in a mixing bowl until light and fluffy. Add the eggs, flour, grated onion, parsley and chives and mix well. Combine the mixture with the potatoes and beat until blended. Do not overbeat. Spoon into a baking dish. Top with the onions. Bake for 30 minutes.

Yield 10 to 12 servings

Becky Wyatt, President 1974–1975

Tip: *If the potatoes become too sticky when beating them, beat in a small amount of evaporated milk.*

Neighbor Tater Stuff

8   potatoes
1 1/2 cups mayonnaise
1   cup sour cream
1 1/2 teaspoons horseradish
1   teaspoon celery seeds
1/2 teaspoon salt
2   onions, finely chopped, or 1 package frozen chives
1   cup chopped fresh parsley
    Salt to taste

Cook the potatoes in boiling water to cover in a large saucepan until tender; drain. Peel the potatoes and cut into 1/8-inch slices. Combine the mayonnaise, sour cream, horseradish, celery seeds and 1/2 teaspoon salt in a bowl and mix well. Combine the onions and parsley in a small bowl. Arrange a layer of potatoes in a large serving bowl. Season lightly with salt. Spread some of the sour cream mixture over the potatoes. Sprinkle with some of the onion mixture. Repeat the layering process until all ingredients are used, ending with the onion mixture. Chill, covered, for 8 hours or longer before serving. Do not stir. This is better when made a day in advance.

Serves 8 to 10

Tip: This was the most requested recipe from our first cookbook.

Baked Spinach and Artichokes

3   (10-ounce) packages frozen chopped
     spinach, thawed and drained
1/2 cup (1 stick) butter, softened
8   ounces cream cheese, softened
1   tablespoon lemon juice
1/2 teaspoon salt
1/4 teaspoon nutmeg
1   (14-ounce) can artichoke hearts,
     drained and sliced
     Ritz crackers, crushed

Preheat the oven to 400 degrees. Squeeze the excess liquid from the spinach and place in a large bowl. Cream the butter and cream cheese in a mixing bowl. Add the lemon juice, salt and nutmeg and mix well. Add to the spinach and mix well. Arrange the artichoke hearts in a greased 11×13-inch baking dish. Spread the spinach mixture over the artichoke hearts. Top with the cracker crumbs. Bake for 20 minutes.

Serves 8

Roma Amos, President 1966–1967

Spinach with Raisins and Pine Nuts

1/3 cup raisins
3   pounds fresh spinach
2   tablespoons extra-virgin olive oil
2   garlic cloves, minced
1/3 cup toasted pine nuts
1/2 teaspoon salt

Soak the raisins in a small amount of warm water for 10 minutes; drain. Remove and discard the coarse stems from the spinach. Steam the spinach in a small amount of water in a saucepan over medium-high heat for 2 to 3 minutes or until tender; drain. Let cool and pat dry with a paper towel. Heat the olive oil in a large skillet over medium heat. Add the garlic and sauté until the garlic begins to turn opaque. Add the spinach and cook for 1 minute, stirring frequently. Add the raisins, pine nuts and salt and mix well. Adjust the seasonings to taste. Cook for 3 minutes, stirring frequently. Serve immediately.

Serves 4

SPINACH PIE

CHEDDAR CHEESE CRUST

1/2 cup(1 stick) margarine or
   butter, melted
1 cup all-purpose flour
1 teaspoon dry mustard
1 teaspoon salt
1 cup (4 ounces) shredded sharp
   New York Cheddar cheese

FILLING

1 (10-ounce) package frozen chopped
   spinach, thawed and drained
2 eggs, lightly beaten
1 cup skim milk
1 cup chopped sweet onion
1 (4-ounce) can chopped
   mushrooms, drained
1 teaspoon nutmeg
1 teaspoon salt
   Dash of white pepper
1 cup (4 ounces) shredded sharp
   New York Cheddar cheese

For the crust, combine the margarine, flour, dry mustard, salt and cheese in a bowl and mix well. Press evenly over the bottom and up the side of a 10-inch deep-dish nonstick pie plate.

For the filling, preheat the oven to 400 degrees. Combine the spinach, eggs, milk, onion, mushrooms, nutmeg, salt and white pepper in a bowl and mix well. Spoon the mixture into the prepared crust. Bake for 15 minutes. Reduce the oven temperature to 350 degrees. Sprinkle the cheese over the filling. Bake for 25 minutes. Turn the oven off and let the pie stand in the oven for 15 minutes.

Serves 8

Cheesy Baked Spinach

2   (10-ounce) packages frozen chopped
    spinach, thawed and drained
2   eggs
2   (10-ounce) cans cream of
    mushroom soup
2   cups (8 ounces) shredded
    Cheddar cheese
1/2 cup bread crumbs
1   tablespoon butter
    Paprika

Preheat the oven to 350 degrees. Squeeze
the excess liquid from the spinach. Mix the
spinach, eggs, soup and cheese in a bowl.
Spoon into a 2-quart baking dish. Sprinkle
with the bread crumbs and dot with the
butter. Sprinkle with paprika. Bake for
30 minutes or until bubbly.

Serves 8

Judy Mendenhall, President 1976–1977

Posh Squash

2   pounds yellow squash, sliced
1   cup mayonnaise
1   cup (4 ounces) grated
    Parmesan cheese
1   small Vidalia onion or other
    sweet onion, chopped
2   eggs, beaten
1/2 teaspoon salt
1/4 teaspoon pepper
1/2 cup soft bread crumbs
1   tablespoon butter, melted

Combine the squash with boiling salted
water to cover in a saucepan and cook,
covered, for 10 to 15 minutes or until
tender; drain. Let stand until cool. Preheat
the oven to 350 degrees. Combine the
mayonnaise, cheese, onion, eggs, salt and
pepper in a bowl and mix well. Add the
squash and stir gently. Spoon into a lightly
greased 1 1/2-quart baking dish. Combine the
bread crumbs and butter in a small bowl.
Top the squash mixture with the bread
crumbs. Bake for 30 minutes.

Serves 6 to 8

SQUASH CASSEROLE

3   cups sliced summer squash
1/4 cup sour cream, at room temperature
1   tablespoon butter, melted
1   tablespoon shredded Cheddar cheese
1/2 teaspoon salt
1/8 teaspoon paprika
1   egg yolk, beaten
1   tablespoon chopped chives
1/2 cup bread crumbs
1/2 cup (2 ounces) shredded
    Cheddar cheese
2   tablespoons butter, softened

Simmer the squash in water to cover in a saucepan until tender; drain. Preheat the oven to 350 degrees. Combine the sour cream, 1 tablespoon butter, 1 tablespoon cheese, the salt and paprika in a saucepan and cook over low heat until the cheese is melted, stirring constantly. Stir in the egg yolk and chives. Add the squash and mix gently. Spoon the mixture into a buttered baking dish. Sprinkle with the bread crumbs and 1/2 cup cheese. Dot with 2 tablespoons butter. Bake for 25 to 30 minutes or until bubbly and browned.

Serves 6 to 8

SQUASH SOUFFLÉ

2   pounds yellow squash, sliced
1   onion, grated
2   eggs, beaten
2   cups thick white sauce
2   cups (8 ounces) shredded New York
    Cheddar cheese
    Salt and pepper to taste
    Bread crumbs

Cook the squash and onion in water to cover in a saucepan until tender; drain and mash. Combine with the eggs, white sauce, cheese, salt and pepper in a bowl and mix well. Spoon the mixture into the top of a double boiler. Cook over simmering water for 1 hour, stirring occasionally. Preheat the oven to 375 degrees. Spoon the mixture into a baking dish. Top with bread crumbs. Bake until hot and browned.

Serves 6

Sweet Potato Soufflé

1   (17-ounce) can sweet potatoes
2   eggs
1   (5-ounce) can evaporated milk
1/2 cup sugar
1   teaspoon vanilla extract

Preheat the oven to 350 degrees. Combine the undrained sweet potatoes, eggs, evaporated milk, sugar and vanilla in a blender and process until blended. Pour into a buttered baking dish. Bake for 45 minutes or until set.

Serves 4

Allison Forrester, President 1996–1997

Fresh Tomato and Vidalia Onion Tart

1   (1-crust) pie pastry
8   ounces mozzarella cheese, shredded
2   tablespoons chopped fresh basil
4   tomatoes, cut into 1/2-inch slices
1   large Vidalia onion, sliced
1/2 teaspoon salt
1/4 teaspoon pepper
1/4 cup extra-virgin olive oil
    Basil leaves (optional)

Preheat the oven to 400 degrees. Fit the pie pastry into a tart pan. Top with the cheese. Sprinkle with the chopped basil. Arrange the tomatoes and onion over the cheese. Sprinkle with the salt and pepper. Drizzle with the olive oil. Bake for 30 to 40 minutes or until hot and bubbly. Garnish with basil leaves. Serve hot.

Serves 8

The photograph for this recipe appears on page 120.

Stove-Top Zucchini

1   tablespoon butter
1   zucchini, sliced
1   onion, sliced and slices separated
     into rings
2   tomatoes, sliced
     Salt and pepper to taste
1   cup (4 ounces) shredded Cheddar
     cheese

Melt the butter in a skillet. Arrange the zucchini in the skillet. Top with the onion and tomatoes. Season with salt and pepper. Cook, covered, over medium heat until the zucchini and onion are tender-crisp. Turn the heat off. Sprinkle with the cheese and let stand, covered, until the cheese melts. Serve immediately.

Serves 4

Doris Dowdy, President 1973–1974

Zucchini and Yellow Squash with Gruyère

1   pound yellow squash, grated
1   pound zucchini, grated
2   teaspoons salt
1   onion, finely chopped
1   large garlic clove, chopped
2   tablespoons olive oil
2   tablespoons butter
1   cup heavy cream or whipping cream
1/2   cup (2 ounces) shredded
     Gruyère cheese
     Salt and pepper to taste
1   sleeve crackers, crushed
1/4   cup (1 ounce) grated Parmesan cheese
1/2   cup (1 stick) butter, melted
     Tomato halves (optional)

Place the squash and zucchini in a colander and sprinkle with 2 teaspoons salt. Let drain for 30 minutes. Squeeze the excess moisture from the mixture. Preheat the oven to 350 degrees. Sauté the onion and garlic in the olive oil and 2 tablespoons butter in a skillet until soft. Add the squash mixture and cook for 2 minutes, stirring occasionally. Stir in the cream, Gruyère cheese, salt and pepper and cook until most of the cream is absorbed, stirring occasionally. Spoon into a baking dish or into tomato halves arranged on a baking sheet. Sprinkle with the cracker crumbs and Parmesan cheese. Drizzle with the butter. Bake until bubbly.

Serves 8

Casserole of Vegetables au Gratin

1/4   cup (1/2 stick) butter
3/4   cup coarsely chopped green bell pepper
1   garlic clove, chopped
2/3   cup milk
1/4   cup all-purpose flour
1/4   teaspoon sugar
3/4   teaspoon salt
1/8   teaspoon pepper
1/8   teaspoon basil
1/8   teaspoon oregano
1/2   cup (2 ounces) shredded
      Cheddar cheese
1   cup chopped tomatoes, drained
1   (10-ounce) package frozen
      corn, thawed
2   (16-ounce) cans whole onions, drained
1/2   cup (2 ounces) shredded
      Cheddar cheese

Preheat the oven to 350 degrees. Melt the butter in a saucepan. Add the bell pepper and garlic and cook over medium-low heat until the bell pepper is tender-crisp. Stir in the milk, flour, sugar, salt, pepper, basil and oregano. Cook until the sauce begins to thicken, stirring constantly. Remove from the heat and add 1/2 cup cheese, stirring until melted. Add the tomatoes and cook until the sauce is thickened. Stir in the corn and onions. Spoon into a 2-quart baking dish. Sprinkle with 1/2 cup cheese. Bake for 50 minutes.

Serves 6

ROASTED VEGETABLES

5	large russet potatoes, cubed
3	large sweet potatoes, peeled and cubed
1	zucchini, peeled and cubed
2	tablespoons olive oil
2	red onions, cut into chunks
2	red or green bell peppers, cut into chunks
1	tablespoon olive oil
	Salt and pepper to taste

Preheat the oven to 400 degrees. Toss the potatoes, sweet potatoes and zucchini with 2 tablespoons olive oil in a bowl until the vegetables are coated. Spread the vegetables in a single layer in 2 shallow baking pans. Roast for 10 minutes.

Toss the onions and bell peppers with 1 tablespoon olive oil in a bowl until coated. Add to the potato mixture and sprinkle with salt and pepper. Roast for 20 minutes or until the vegetables are browned and beginning to dehydrate. Serve hot or cold.

Serves 10 to 12

The photograph for this recipe appears on page 79.

VEGETABLE RELISH

2   (20-ounce) cans French-style green
      beans, drained
2   (20-ounce) cans tiny garden peas,
      drained
1   (11-ounce) can white Shoe Peg
      corn, drained
1   (2-ounce) jar pimentos
1 1/2 cups chopped celery
1   cup chopped green or red bell pepper
2   tablespoons chopped Vidalia onion or
      other sweet onion
1   cup apple cider vinegar
1/2   cup vegetable oil
2   tablespoons water
      Pepper to taste
3/4   cup sugar, or more to taste

Combine the green beans, peas, corn,
pimentos, celery, bell pepper and onion in a
large bowl. Combine the vinegar, oil, water,
pepper and sugar in a bowl and whisk until
the sugar is dissolved and the mixture is
blended. Pour over the vegetables and toss
gently. Chill, covered, for 8 hours or longer.
Serve with grilled chicken and corn on the
cob. This will keep in the refrigerator for
several days.

Serves 10 to 12

CRISP SWEET PICKLES

1   (32-ounce) jar whole kosher dill
      pickles, drained
1 1/4 cups sugar
3   tablespoons apple cider vinegar
1   tablespoon dried minced onion
1   tablespoon celery seeds

Cut the pickles into 1/2-inch slices and place
in the pickle jar. Add the sugar, vinegar,
onion and celery seeds and replace the lid.
Shake until the pickles are coated. Store in
the refrigerator for 1 week or longer,
shaking occasionally.

Makes 1 quart

Quick-and-Easy Refrigerator Pickles

1   gallon cucumbers, peeled and sliced
2   cups sugar
2   cups apple cider vinegar
2   tablespoons salt
3/4   teaspoon mustard seeds
3/4   teaspoon celery seeds

Combine the cucumbers, sugar, vinegar, salt, mustard seeds and celery seeds in a large jar with a tight-fitting lid. Shake to coat the cucumbers. Store in the refrigerator for up to 1 week, shaking occasionally.

Makes 1 gallon

Sweet-and-Sour Beans

1 1/3 cups each sugar and vinegar
2/3   cup water
3   tablespoons vegetable oil
1   small onion, chopped
2   (10-ounce) packages frozen
       French-style green beans

Bring the first 5 ingredients to a boil in a saucepan over medium-high heat. Boil for 8 to 10 minutes, stirring occasionally. Pour over the green beans in a bowl. Marinate in the refrigerator for 2 to 3 days.

Serves 6 to 8

Brandied Cranberries

1   pound fresh cranberries
2   cups sugar
1/4   cup brandy
1/4   cup sugar

Preheat the oven to 350 degrees. Place the cranberries in a shallow glass baking dish. Sprinkle with 2 cups sugar. Bake, covered, for 1 hour. Drizzle with the brandy and sprinkle with 1/4 cup sugar. Spoon into an airtight container and chill until ready to serve.

Makes about 3 cups

Fran Thomas, President 1956–1957

PINEAPPLE AU GRATIN

1	(15-ounce) can pineapple chunks, drained
1	(15-ounce) can crushed pineapple, drained
1	cup sugar
6	tablespoons self-rising flour
1	to 2 cups (4 to 8 ounces) shredded sharp Cheddar cheese
1	sleeve Ritz crackers, crushed
1/2	cup (1 stick) butter or margarine, melted

Preheat the oven to 350 degrees. Combine the pineapple, sugar, flour and cheese in a bowl and mix well. Spoon into a greased 9×13-inch baking dish. Sprinkle with the cracker crumbs and drizzle with the butter. Bake for 20 to 25 minutes or until the top is golden brown and the mixture is bubbly. Let stand for 10 minutes before serving.

Serves 8

SPICED WINTER FRUIT

1	(17-ounce) can apricots
1	(16-ounce) can pears
1	(16-ounce) can sliced peaches
1	(15-ounce) can pineapple chunks
1	(15-ounce) jar applesauce
1/4	cup sherry
1/2	teaspoon cinnamon
1/8	teaspoon nutmeg
2	tablespoons butter

Drain the apricots, pears, peaches and pineapple, reserving half the juice from each can. Layer half the apricots, half the pears, half the peaches and half the pineapple in a 3-quart baking dish. Preheat the oven to 325 degrees. Heat the applesauce in a saucepan over medium heat for 5 minutes. Add the remaining fruit, reserved juice, sherry, cinnamon and nutmeg and bring to a boil, stirring occasionally. Pour over the fruit in the baking dish. Dot with the butter. Bake for 30 to 45 minutes or until bubbly.

Serves about 8

HOLIDAY CHEESE GRITS

2   cups quick-cooking grits
2   cups (8 ounces) shredded
    Cheddar cheese
1   cup half-and-half
2   tablespoons butter
3   eggs, lightly beaten
    Paprika

Preheat the oven to 325 degrees. Cook the grits in a large saucepan using the package directions. Add the cheese, half-and-half and butter and stir until the cheese is melted. Remove from the heat and let cool slightly. Stir in the eggs. Spoon into an 11×14-inch baking dish. Sprinkle with paprika. Bake for 45 minutes.

Serves 8

Ann Busby, President 1984–1985

MACARONI AND CHEESE

1/4   cup chopped onion
      Margarine
16   ounces elbow macaroni, cooked
      and drained
1   (10-ounce) can cream of
      mushroom soup
1   cup mayonnaise
16   ounces Cheddar cheese, shredded
1   (4-ounce) can mushrooms, drained
      and chopped
1/4   cup chopped pimentos
      Dash of garlic powder
      Ritz crackers, crushed

Preheat the oven to 350 degrees. Brown the onion in margarine in a skillet. Combine the macaroni, soup, mayonnaise, cheese, mushrooms, pimentos, garlic powder and onion in a large bowl and mix well. Spoon into a large baking dish. Top with cracker crumbs. Bake for 25 to 30 minutes.

Serves 8

Lime and Cilantro Butter

1   cup (2 sticks) unsalted butter, softened
3   tablespoons chopped fresh cilantro
     Juice of 2 limes
     Kosher salt or sea salt to taste

Combine the butter, cilantro, lime juice and salt in a bowl and mix well. Shape into a log and wrap with waxed paper. Store in the freezer.

Makes 1 cup

Lemon and Thyme Butter

1   cup (2 sticks) unsalted butter, softened
3   tablespoons chopped fresh thyme
     Juice of 2 lemons
     Kosher salt or sea salt to taste

Combine the butter, thyme, lemon juice and salt in a bowl and mix well. Shape into a log and wrap with waxed paper. Store in the freezer.

Makes 1 cup

Barbecue Sauce with Whiskey

1   cup ketchup
1/2   cup prepared mustard
1/4   cup maple syrup or molasses
1/4   cup Worcestershire sauce
1/4   cup packed brown sugar
1   tablespoon whiskey
1   teaspoon garlic powder
1   teaspoon onion powder
1   teaspoon lemon juice
1/4   to 1/2 teaspoon cayenne pepper

Combine the ketchup, mustard, maple syrup, Worcestershire sauce, brown sugar, whiskey, garlic powder, onion powder, lemon juice and cayenne pepper in a bowl and mix well. Store in the refrigerator in an airtight container.

Makes about 2 1/2 cups

FINISHES

DESSERTS

Cocoa Chiffon Cake with
Seven-Minute Frosting *page 151*

Applesauce Cake

1/2 cup (1 stick) butter or
    margarine, softened
2   cups sugar
2   eggs
2   cups applesauce
2 1/2 cups all-purpose flour
1   tablespoon baking soda
1   tablespoon ground cinnamon
1   teaspoon ground allspice
1   teaspoon ground cloves
2   cups raisins
1   cup chopped nuts
1   cup chopped candied fruit (optional)

Preheat the oven to 325 degrees. Cream the butter and sugar in a mixing bowl until light and fluffy. Beat in the eggs and applesauce. Stir in the flour, baking soda, cinnamon, allspice and cloves. Stir in the raisins, nuts and candied fruit. Spoon into a greased and floured 10-inch tube pan. Bake for 1 1/2 hours or until the cake tests done. Cool in the pan for 10 minutes. Remove the cake to a wire rack to cool completely.

Serves 12 to 16

Southern Jam Cake

1   cup (2 sticks) butter, softened
2   cups sugar
6   eggs
2   cups jam, any flavor or
    combination of flavors
3   cups all-purpose flour
1   teaspoon ground cinnamon
1   teaspoon ground cloves
1   teaspoon baking soda
1/4 teaspoon salt
1   cup buttermilk

Preheat the oven to 325 degrees. Cream the butter and sugar in a large mixing bowl until light and fluffy. Beat in the eggs and jam until blended. Stir together the flour, cinnamon, cloves, baking soda and salt. Add the flour mixture and buttermilk alternately to the batter, beating well after each addition and ending with flour. Pour into a greased and floured 10-inch tube pan. Bake for 1 hour or until the cake tests done. Cool in the pan for 10 minutes. Remove the cake to a wire rack to cool completely. Frost with your favorite icing or glaze, if desired.

Serves 12 to 16

Old-Fashioned Butter Cake with Rich Chocolate Frosting

BUTTER CAKE

1	cup (2 sticks) butter, softened
1/2	cup shortening
2 1/2	cups sugar
2	teaspoons vanilla extract
5	eggs
3	cups all-purpose flour, sifted
1/2	teaspoon baking powder
1/2	teaspoon salt
1	cup milk

RICH CHOCOLATE FROSTING

1	cup (2 sticks) butter, softened
2	ounces unsweetened chocolate, melted
2	ounces semisweet chocolate, melted
4	cups confectioners' sugar, sifted
1/4	cup baking cocoa
1/4	cup milk
2	teaspoons vanilla extract

For the cake, preheat the oven to 350 degrees. Cream the butter and shortening in a large mixing bowl until light and fluffy. Add the sugar gradually, beating well after each addition. Add the vanilla. Beat in the eggs 1 at a time. Stir together the flour, baking powder and salt. Add the flour mixture and milk alternately to the batter, beating well after each addition and beginning and ending with flour. Pour into 3 well-greased and floured 9-inch cake pans or two 10-inch cake pans. Bake for 25 minutes or until the layers test done. Cool in the pans for 10 minutes. Remove the layers to a wire rack to cool completely.

For the frosting, beat the butter in a large mixing bowl until light and fluffy. Beat in the melted chocolate, then the confectioners' sugar, baking cocoa, milk and vanilla until smooth. Spread the frosting between the cooled cake layers and over the side and top of the cake.

Serves 12 to 16

PENNY'S CARAMEL CAKE

VANILLA CAKE

1	cup (2 sticks) butter or margarine, softened
3	cups sugar
5	eggs
3 1/2	cups all-purpose flour
1/2	teaspoon baking powder
1/4	teaspoon salt
1	teaspoon vanilla extract
1 1/4	cups whole milk or evaporated milk

CARAMEL ICING

1	cup (2 sticks) butter
1	pound light brown sugar
1/4	teaspoon salt
2/3	cup evaporated milk
2	cups confectioners' sugar, sifted
2	teaspoons vanilla extract

For the cake, preheat the oven to 350 degrees. Beat the butter and sugar in a large mixing bowl until light and fluffy. Beat in the eggs 1 at a time. Stir together the flour, baking powder and salt. Stir the vanilla into the milk. Add the flour mixture and milk alternately to the batter, beating well after each addition. Pour into a greased and floured 13×18-inch sheet cake pan or three 9- or 10-inch layer cake pans. Bake the sheet pan for 60 minutes; bake the layer pans for 30 minutes or until the cake tests done. Cool the sheet cake in the pan. Cool the layer cakes in the pans for 10 minutes; remove to a wire rack to cool completely.

For the icing, melt the butter in a 2-quart saucepan. Add the brown sugar and salt. Cook over medium heat until the brown sugar dissolves, stirring constantly. Add the evaporated milk gradually, stirring constantly until blended. Bring to a boil; boil gently for 9 minutes without stirring. Remove from the heat and let cool. Beat the confectioners' sugar gradually into the cooked mixture using an electric mixer. Add the vanilla. Beat until caramelized and thickened to the desired consistency. If the icing is too thin, add more confectioners' sugar. If it is too thick, add a few drops of evaporated milk. Spread the icing over the top of the sheet cake or between the cooled layers and over the side and top of the cake.

Serves 12 to 16

Penny Leonard, President 1964–1965

CARROT CAKE WITH CREAM CHEESE ICING

CARROT CAKE

2	cups sugar
1¹/2	cups vegetable oil
4	eggs
2	cups all-purpose flour
2	teaspoons baking powder
2	teaspoons baking soda
2	teaspoons ground cinnamon
1	teaspoon salt
3	cups grated carrots
1	cup pecans, chopped
1	teaspoon vanilla extract

CREAM CHEESE ICING

8	ounces cream cheese, softened
¹/4	cup (¹/2 stick) butter, softened
1	pound confectioners' sugar
1	teaspoon vanilla extract

For the cake, preheat the oven to 325 degrees. Beat the sugar and oil in a large mixing bowl until blended. Beat in the eggs 1 at a time. Sift together the flour, baking powder, baking soda, cinnamon and salt and add to the batter, beating until smooth. Stir in the carrots, pecans and vanilla and mix well. Pour into a greased and floured 9×13-inch cake pan. Bake for 45 minutes or until the cake tests done. Cool completely.

For the icing, beat the cream cheese and butter in a large mixing bowl until light and fluffy. Beat in the confectioners' sugar and vanilla until smooth. Spread over the top of the cooled cake.

Serves 12 to 16

Chocolate Pound Cake with Chocolate Fudge Icing

POUND CAKE

1	cup (2 sticks) butter, softened
1/2	cup shortening
3	cups sugar
5	eggs
3	cups all-purpose flour
5	tablespoons baking cocoa
1/2	teaspoon baking powder
1/4	teaspoon salt
1	cup milk
1	teaspoon vanilla extract

CHOCOLATE FUDGE ICING

3	ounces unsweetened chocolate, melted
3	ounces cream cheese, softened
1/4	cup evaporated milk
1	teaspoon vanilla extract
1/8	teaspoon salt
2	cups confectioners' sugar

For the cake, preheat the oven to 325 degrees. Cream the butter and shortening in a large mixing bowl until light and fluffy. Add the sugar and beat until smooth. Beat in the eggs 1 at a time. Sift together the flour, baking cocoa, baking powder and salt. Add the flour mixture and the milk alternately to the batter, beating well after each addition and ending with milk. Stir in the vanilla. Pour into a greased and floured 10-inch tube pan. Bake for 1 to 1 1/2 hours or until a wooden pick inserted in the center comes out clean. Cool in the pan for 15 minutes. Remove the cake to a wire rack to cool completely.

For the icing, combine the melted chocolate, cream cheese, evaporated milk, vanilla and salt in a mixing bowl and beat until blended. Beat in the confectioners' sugar until smooth. Chill if the icing is too thin; then beat again and spread over the cooled cake.

Serves 12 to 16

Margaret Hart, President 1952–1953

Chocolate Sheet Cake

CAKE

2   cups all-purpose flour

2   cups sugar

1   teaspoon baking soda

1/2   teaspoon salt

1/2   cup sour cream, at room temperature

1   cup (2 sticks) butter

1   cup water

1/4   cup baking cocoa

ICING

1   pound confectioners' sugar

1   teaspoon vanilla extract

1/2   cup (1 stick) butter

6   tablespoons milk

1/4   cup baking cocoa

1   to 1 1/2 cups chopped pecans or walnuts or a combination

For the cake, preheat the oven to 350 degrees. Place the flour, sugar, baking soda, salt and sour cream in a large mixing bowl. Melt the butter with the water and baking cocoa in a saucepan and bring to a boil, stirring occasionally. Remove from the heat and add to the flour mixture, beating until smooth. Pour into a greased and floured 9×13-inch or larger sheet cake pan. Bake for 20 minutes or until the cake tests done. Let cool.

For the icing, combine the confectioners' sugar and vanilla in a large bowl. Melt the butter with the milk and baking cocoa in a saucepan. Bring to a boil, stirring constantly. Remove from the heat and add to the confectioners' sugar mixture. Stir until smooth. Spread over the cake while still warm. Sprinkle with the pecans.

Serves 12 to 16

Barbara Coughlin, President 1992–1993

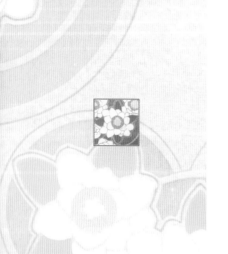

Triple Chocolate Sour Cream Bundt Cake

1	(2-layer) package chocolate or devil's food pudding-in cake mix
1	(4-ounce) package chocolate or devil's food instant pudding mix
1/2	cup granulated sugar
1/2	cup vegetable oil
1/2	cup water
4	eggs
1	cup sour cream
2	cups (12 ounces) semisweet chocolate chips Confectioners' sugar

Preheat the oven to 350 degrees. Whisk together the cake mix, pudding mix and granulated sugar in a large bowl. Add the oil, water, eggs and sour cream and whisk until smooth and blended. Stir in the chocolate chips. Pour into a greased and floured 12-cup bundt pan. Bake for 50 to 55 minutes or until the cake tests done. Cool in the pan for 10 minutes. Remove the cake to a wire rack to cool completely. Sprinkle with confectioners' sugar.

Serves 12 to 16

Cocoa Chiffon Cake with Seven-Minute Frosting

CAKE

3/4 cup boiling water
1/2 cup baking cocoa
1 3/4 cups cake flour
1 3/4 cups sugar
1 1/2 teaspoons baking soda
1 teaspoon salt
1/2 cup vegetable oil
7 egg yolks
2 teaspoons vanilla extract
1 cup egg whites (7 or 8 large eggs),
at room temperature
1/2 teaspoon cream of tartar

SEVEN-MINUTE FROSTING

2 egg whites, at room temperature
1 1/3 cups sugar
Dash of cream of tartar
2 to 3 tablespoons water
2/3 cup miniature marshmallows
Vanilla extract to taste

For the cake, preheat the oven to 325 degrees. Pour the water over the baking cocoa in a small bowl and mix well; cool. Sift together the flour, sugar, baking soda and salt in a large bowl. Make a well in the center of the mixture. Add the oil, unbeaten egg yolks, vanilla and cooled cocoa mixture and mix well. Combine the egg whites and cream of tartar in a large mixing bowl and beat until stiff peaks form. Fold in the chocolate mixture gently. Pour into an ungreased 10-inch tube pan. Bake for 1 hour or until the cake tests done. Invert the pan immediately and cool completely. Loosen the cake from the pan and turn onto a serving plate. Spread the side and top of the cake with the frosting.

For the frosting, combine the the first 5 ingredients in the top of a double boiler placed over boiling water. Cook for 5 to 7 minutes, beating constantly until glossy stiff peaks form. Remove from the heat and add the vanilla.

Serves 12

Evie Cottam, President 2004–2005

The photograph for this recipe appears on page 142.

Italian Cream Cake

CAKE

1/2   cup (1 stick) butter, softened
1/2   cup shortening
2   cups sugar
5   egg yolks, at room temperature
1   teaspoon baking soda
1   cup buttermilk
2   cups all-purpose flour
1   (3-ounce) can flaked coconut
1/2   cup pecans, finely chopped
1   teaspoon vanilla extract
5   egg whites, at room temperature

ORANGE CREAM CHEESE FROSTING

8   ounces cream cheese, softened
1/2   cup (1 stick) butter, softened
2   tablespoons frozen orange juice concentrate, thawed
1   teaspoon vanilla extract
1   pound confectioners' sugar

For the cake, preheat the oven to 350 degrees. Cream the butter, shortening and sugar in a large mixing bowl until light and fluffy. Beat in the egg yolks until smooth. Stir the baking soda into the buttermilk. Add the flour and buttermilk alternately to the batter, mixing well after each addition and beginning and ending with flour. Stir in the coconut, pecans and vanilla. Beat the egg whites in a deep mixing bowl until stiff peaks form. Fold into the batter. Pour into 3 greased and floured 9-inch cake pans. Bake for 25 minutes or until the layers test done. Cool in the pans for 10 minutes. Remove the layers to a wire rack to cool completely.

For the frosting, beat the cream cheese and butter in a mixing bowl until light and fluffy. Add the orange juice concentrate and the vanilla. Add the confectioners' sugar gradually, beating constantly until smooth. Spread between the cooled layers and over the side and top of the cake; chill. Store the cake in the refrigerator.

Serves 12 to 16

BEST LEMON CAKE

CAKE

1	cup (2 sticks) butter, softened
1/2	cup shortening
3	cups sugar
1/4	teaspoon salt
2	teaspoons grated lemon zest
5	eggs
2	cups all-purpose flour
1	cup milk
1	cup all-purpose flour
1/2	teaspoon baking powder

LEMON FROSTING

1/4	cup (1/2 stick) butter, softened
	Grated zest of 1 1/2 lemons
1	pound confectioners' sugar
	Juice of 1 1/2 lemons

For the cake, cream the butter, shortening, sugar and salt in a large mixing bowl until light and fluffy. Add the lemon zest. Beat in the eggs 1 at a time. Add 2 cups flour and the milk alternately, mixing well after each addition and beginning and ending with flour. Stir together 1 cup flour and the baking powder and stir into the batter all at once. Pour into a well-greased and floured 10-inch tube pan. Place in a cold oven; set the oven temperature to 325 degrees. Bake for 1 1/2 hours or until the cake tests done. Cool in the pan for 6 to 7 minutes. Turn the hot cake onto the bottom of a cake keeper lined with a paper towel; place a paper towel on top of the cake. Cover with the cake keeper lid to retain the moisture. Cool completely.

For the frosting, beat the butter and lemon zest in a mixing bowl until light and fluffy. Beat in the confectioners' sugar until blended. Beat in enough lemon juice to make of spreading consistency. Uncover the cooled cake and frost the side and top of the cake.

Serves 12 to 16

Caryl Adams, President 2000–2002

Easy Lemon Pound Cake

1 (3-ounce) package lemon gelatin
2/3 cup hot water
1 (2-layer) package yellow cake mix
2/3 cup vegetable oil
4 eggs
1/2 teaspoon vanilla extract
1/2 teaspoon lemon flavoring

Preheat the oven to 325 degrees. Dissolve the gelatin in the hot water in a large mixing bowl. Add the cake mix and beat well. Beat in the oil. Beat in the eggs 1 at a time. Add the vanilla and lemon flavoring and mix well. Pour into a greased and floured 10-inch tube pan. Bake for 1 hour or until the cake tests done. Cool in the pan for 10 minutes. Remove the cake to a wire rack to cool completely.

Serves 12 to 16

Lore Fariss, President 1999–2000

Orange Slice Cake

1 cup (2 sticks) butter, softened
2 cups granulated sugar
4 eggs
1 teaspoon baking soda
1/4 cup buttermilk
31/2 cups all-purpose flour
1 pound dates, chopped
1 pound orange slice candy, chopped
2 cups pecans, chopped
1 (3-ounce) can flaked coconut
1 cup fresh orange juice
2 cups confectioners' sugar

Preheat the oven to 250 degrees. Cream the butter and granulated sugar in a large mixing bowl until light and fluffy. Beat in the eggs 1 at a time. Add the baking soda to the buttermilk, stirring until dissolved. Add to the butter mixture. Place the flour in a large bowl and add the dates, candy, pecans and coconut, stirring to coat well with the flour. Add the butter mixture and mix well with your hands. Spread in a greased and floured 9×13-inch cake pan. Bake for 21/2 hours or until the cake tests done. Combine the orange juice and confectioners' sugar in a bowl, stirring until smooth. Poke holes in the hot cake with a wooden pick or fork and pour the orange juice mixture over the top. Cool completely.

Serves 12 to 16

Oatmeal Cake with Coconut Frosting

CAKE

1 1/2   cups boiling water
1   cup quick-cooking oats
1   cup packed brown sugar
1   cup granulated sugar
1/2   cup vegetable oil
2   eggs
1 1/2   cups all-purpose flour
1 1/2   teaspoons ground cinnamon
1   teaspoon baking soda
1   teaspoon salt

COCONUT FROSTING

1/2   cup (1 stick) butter or margarine
1   cup packed light brown sugar
1   teaspoon vanilla extract
1   (3-ounce) can flaked coconut
1   cup chopped nuts

For the cake, preheat the oven to 350 degrees. Pour the boiling water over the oats in a large bowl and set aside to cool. Beat the brown sugar, granulated sugar, oil and eggs in a large mixing bowl until blended. Stir together the flour, cinnamon, baking soda and salt and add to the sugar mixture, mixing well. The batter will be stiff. Add the oatmeal and mix well. Pour into a greased and floured 9×13-inch cake pan. Bake for 35 to 40 minutes or until the cake tests done.

For the frosting, combine the butter and brown sugar in a large saucepan and bring to a boil. Reduce the heat and cook until the mixture has thickened, stirring constantly. Remove from the heat and stir in the vanilla, coconut and nuts. Spread over the hot cake.

Serves 15

Fresh Peach Cake

3   eggs
1 3/4 cups sugar
1   cup vegetable oil
1 1/2 cups all-purpose flour
1   teaspoon baking soda
1   teaspoon salt
1   teaspoon ground cinnamon
2   cups sliced fresh peaches
1/2 cup pecans, chopped
1/2 cup all-purpose flour
    Whipped cream (optional)

Preheat the oven to 375 degrees. Beat the eggs in a large mixing bowl until frothy. Beat in the sugar and oil until smooth. Stir together 1 1/2 cups flour, baking soda, salt and cinnamon and add to the sugar mixture. Beat at low speed just until blended. The batter will be thick. Combine the peaches, pecans and 1/2 cup flour in a bowl and toss to coat. Fold into the batter. Spoon into a greased and floured 9×13-inch cake pan. Bake for 40 to 50 minutes or until a wooden pick inserted in the center comes out clean. Cool completely. Cut into squares to serve. Garnish each serving with a dollop of whipped cream.

Serves 12 to 16

PINEAPPLE POUND CAKE

CAKE

1	cup (2 sticks) butter, softened
1/2	cup shortening
2 3/4	cups sugar
1	cup all-purpose flour
1	teaspoon baking powder
6	eggs
1/4	cup milk
3/4	cup crushed pineapple, drained
2	cups all-purpose flour
1	teaspoon vanilla extract

GLAZE

1/4	cup (1/2 stick) butter
1	cup crushed pineapple, undrained
1 1/2	cups confectioners' sugar

For the cake, preheat the oven to 325 degrees. Beat the butter, shortening and sugar until light and fluffy. Sift together 1 cup flour and the baking powder and add to the sugar mixture. Add the eggs, milk and pineapple and mix well. Add 2 cups flour and the vanilla and stir until combined. Pour into a greased and floured 10-inch bundt pan. Bake for 1 1/2 hours or until the cake tests done.

For the glaze, melt the butter with the pineapple in a saucepan. Cook for 2 minutes, stirring constantly. Stir in the confectioners' sugar until combined. Pour over the cake while still warm. Cool completely before serving.

Serves 12 to 16

Pumpkin Cake Roll

CAKE

3	eggs
1	cup sugar
2/3	(15-ounce) can pumpkin
3/4	cup all-purpose flour
1	teaspoon baking soda
1/2	teaspoon ground cinnamon

FILLING

8	ounces cream cheese, softened
5	tablespoons butter or margarine, softened
1	cup confectioners' sugar
1	teaspoon vanilla extract
	Additional confectioners' sugar

For the cake, preheat the oven to 375 degrees. Beat the eggs in a large mixing bowl. Add the sugar, pumpkin, flour, baking soda and cinnamon and mix well. Grease a 10×15-inch jelly roll pan and line with waxed paper; grease the waxed paper and dust with flour. Pour the batter into the prepared pan. It will be a very thin layer. Bake for 10 to 15 minutes or until a wooden pick inserted in the center comes out clean. Immediately invert the cake onto a clean tea towel and gently peel off the waxed paper. Roll up with the towel, starting at 1 long side. Cool for 30 minutes.

For the filling, beat the cream cheese and butter in a mixing bowl until light and fluffy. Add 1 cup confectioners' sugar and the vanilla and beat until smooth. Unroll the cake and remove the towel. Spread the cake with the filling and roll up. Dust with confectioners' sugar and arrange seam side down on a serving platter. Chill.

Serves 8 to 10

Tip: The cake roll can be frozen.

Shoo-Fly Cake

2   cups boiling water
1   cup molasses
1   tablespoon baking soda
4   cups all-purpose flour
2   cups packed brown sugar
3/4 cup vegetable oil
1/4 teaspoon salt

Preheat the oven to 350 degrees. Combine the water, molasses and baking soda in a large mixing bowl and mix well. Combine the flour, brown sugar, oil and salt in a large bowl and mix until crumbly. Reserve 1 cup of the crumb mixture. Add the remaining crumb mixture to the molasses mixture and mix well. Pour into a greased 9×13-inch cake pan. Bake for 20 minutes. Remove from the oven and sprinkle the reserved crumb mixture evenly over the top. Bake for 30 minutes longer or until the cake tests done. Cool for 1 hour before serving.

Serves 12 to 16

Real Moravian Sugar Cake

1   envelope dry yeast (not instant)
1/2 cup lukewarm water
1   cup hot unseasoned mashed potatoes
     (made from fresh potatoes;
     1 cup potato cooking water reserved)
1   cup granulated sugar
1/2 cup shortening
1/4 cup (1/2 stick) butter, softened
1   teaspoon salt
2   eggs, beaten
3   cups all-purpose flour
     Additional butter, softened
     Brown sugar and ground cinnamon
     Heavy cream or whipping cream

Dissolve the yeast in the water in a small bowl. Combine the mashed potatoes, granulated sugar, shortening, 1/4 cup butter and the salt in a large bowl and mix well. Cool to lukewarm. Add the yeast mixture and reserved potato water and mix well. Cover and let rise until spongy. Add the eggs. Add the flour 1/2 cup at a time, stirring to make a soft dough. Do not knead. Let rise until doubled in bulk. Punch down and divide the dough in half. Spread each half in a greased 10×15-inch cake pan and let rise. Preheat the oven to 375 degrees. Make indentations in the dough with your fingers. Fill the indentations with softened butter and brown sugar. Sprinkle with cinnamon and drizzle with cream. Bake for 20 minutes. Serve warm.

Serves 24 to 30

Black Bottom Cupcakes

8	ounces cream cheese, softened
1	egg
1/3	cup sugar
1/8	teaspoon salt
1	cup (6 ounces) miniature chocolate chips
1 1/2	cups all-purpose flour
1	cup sugar
1/4	cup baking cocoa
1	teaspoon baking soda
1/2	teaspoon salt
1	cup water
1/3	cup vegetable oil
1	tablespoon vinegar
1	teaspoon vanilla extract
	Additional sugar
	Chopped nuts

Preheat the oven to 350 degrees. Beat the cream cheese, egg, 1/3 cup sugar and 1/8 teaspoon salt in a mixing bowl until light and fluffy. Stir in the chocolate chips. Stir together the flour, 1 cup sugar, the baking cocoa, baking soda and 1/2 teaspoon salt in a large bowl. Add the water, oil, vinegar and vanilla and mix well. Fill greased or paper-lined muffin cups 1/3 full with the flour mixture. Top each with 1 teaspoon of the cream cheese mixture. Sprinkle with sugar and nuts. Bake for 30 to 35 minutes; cool.

Makes 18 to 24 cupcakes

Fruit and Nut Bars

2	cups nuts, chopped
1/2	cup (1 stick) butter, softened
1 1/2	cups packed dark brown sugar
2	eggs
1	cup all-purpose flour
1	teaspoon vanilla extract
8	ounces candied cherries, chopped
10	ounces candied pineapple, diced

Preheat the oven to 300 degrees. Spread the nuts evenly in a well-greased and floured 9×13-inch baking pan. Cream the butter and brown sugar in a large mixing bowl until light and fluffy. Beat in the eggs, flour and vanilla until combined. Pour over the nuts and press into the pan using a damp hand. Sprinkle the cherries and pineapple over the dough and press down lightly. Bake for 1 hour or until a wooden pick inserted in the center comes out clean. Cool and cut into bars.

Makes 24 bars

Tip: You may substitute 6 ounces cherry-flavored sweetened dried cranberries for the candied cherries, if desired.

Lemon Cheesecake Cookies

1/2 cup (1 stick) butter, softened
1/4 cup sugar
1   teaspoon grated lemon zest
1/4 teaspoon salt
1 1/4 cups all-purpose flour
3   tablespoons fresh lemon juice
16   ounces cream cheese, softened
2/3 cup sugar
2   eggs

Line a 9×9-inch baking pan with foil, extending 2 inches beyond the sides of the pan. Cream the butter, 1/4 cup sugar, 1/2 teaspoon of the lemon zest and the salt in a mixing bowl. Add the flour gradually, stirring until blended. Add 1 tablespoon of the lemon juice, stirring just until the dough holds together. Press onto the bottom of the prepared pan and chill for 15 minutes. Preheat the oven to 350 degrees. Bake for 20 to 25 minutes or until golden brown. Beat the cream cheese and 2/3 cup sugar in a mixing bowl until fluffy. Beat in the eggs, remaining 1/2 teaspoon lemon zest and remaining lemon juice until smooth. Pour over the crust. Bake for 35 to 40 minutes or until puffed and firm to the touch. Cool completely; chill. Let stand at room temperature for 1 hour. Lift the cheesecake from the pan with the foil. Remove the foil. Cut into bars and then cut each bar diagonally into 2 triangles.

Makes 18 triangles

Caramel Brownies

1   (14-ounce) package caramels
1/3 cup evaporated milk
1   (2-layer) package German chocolate cake mix
1/2 cup (1 stick) margarine, melted
1/3 cup evaporated milk
1   cup nuts, chopped
1   cup (6 ounces) semisweet chocolate chips

Preheat the oven to 350 degrees. Combine the caramels and 1/3 cup evaporated milk in a heavy saucepan. Cook over low heat until melted, stirring constantly. Remove from the heat and let cool. Combine the cake mix, margarine, 1/3 cup evaporated milk and the nuts in a large bowl, stirring just until combined. Press half the dough onto the bottom of a greased and floured 9×13-inch baking dish. Bake for 8 minutes. Remove from the oven and spread the caramel mixture evenly over the crust. Sprinkle the chocolate chips evenly over the caramel. Crumble the remaining dough over the top. Return to the oven and bake for 15 to 18 minutes. Cool for 1 hour or longer. Cut into small bars.

Makes 24 to 36 brownies

Fudgy Cream Cheese Brownies

1   (2-layer) package butter fudge cake mix
1   egg
1/2 cup (1 stick) butter, melted
1/2 cup pecans, chopped
8   ounces cream cheese, softened
3   eggs
1   pound confectioners' sugar
1/2 cup pecans, chopped

Preheat the oven to 350 degrees. Combine the cake mix, 1 egg and the butter in a large bowl and mix well by hand. Stir in 1/2 cup pecans. The dough will be very stiff. Press onto the bottom of a greased and floured 9×13-inch baking pan. Beat the cream cheese and 3 eggs in a large mixing bowl until light and fluffy. Beat in the confectioners' sugar until smooth. Stir in 1/2 cup pecans. Press indentations in the brownie layer in the pan with a large spoon. Pour the cream cheese mixture over the top and spread evenly. Bake for 35 to 40 minutes. Let stand until cool.

Makes 24 brownies

Penny Honeycutt, President 1977–1978

Mint Brownies

1   (21-ounce) package brownie mix
1/2 cup (1 stick) butter, softened
2   cups confectioners' sugar
1/4 cup crème de menthe
6   tablespoons butter
3/4 cup (4 1/2 ounces) semisweet chocolate chips

Prepare and bake the brownies in a 9×13-inch baking pan using the package directions for fudge-like brownies; cool. Chill in the refrigerator. Beat 1/2 cup butter, the confectioners' sugar and crème de menthe in a mixing bowl until smooth. Spread over the cold brownies and chill. Melt 6 tablespoons butter and the chocolate chips in a small saucepan over low heat, stirring until smooth. Spread the chocolate mixture evenly over the mint layer. Chill completely. Cut into small bars.

Makes 24 to 36 brownies

Iced Cake Brownies

BROWNIES

1 1/2 cups (3 sticks) margarine

1/4 cup baking cocoa

1 cup water

1/2 cup buttermilk

2 eggs

1 teaspoon vanilla extract

2 cups sugar

2 cups all-purpose flour

1 teaspoon baking soda

ICING

1/2 cup (1 stick) margarine

1/3 cup milk

1/4 cup baking cocoa

1 pound confectioners' sugar, sifted

1 teaspoon vanilla extract

1 cup nuts, chopped

For the brownies, preheat the oven to 400 degrees. Melt the margarine with the baking cocoa and water in a large saucepan. Bring to a boil. Remove from the heat and add the buttermilk. Whisk the eggs in a bowl until frothy. Whisk in 2 tablespoons of the hot cocoa mixture. Whisk the eggs into the cocoa mixture. Add the vanilla. Stir together the sugar, flour and baking soda and add to the cocoa mixture, beating until smooth. The batter will be thin. Pour into a greased and floured 10×15-inch baking pan. Bake for 20 minutes or until the brownies test done; cool.

For the icing, melt the margarine with the milk and the baking cocoa in a saucepan over low heat, stirring constantly. Bring to a boil and boil for 1 1/2 minutes. Remove from the heat and add the confectioners' sugar and vanilla. Beat until smooth and of spreading consistency. Stir in the nuts. Spread over the cooled brownie layer. Cut into bars.

Makes 48 brownies

CHOCOLATE CHIP COOKIES

1/3 cup butter, softened
1/3 cup shortening
1/2 cup packed brown sugar
1/2 cup granulated sugar
1   egg
1   teaspoon vanilla extract
11/2 cups all-purpose flour
1/2 teaspoon baking powder
1/2 teaspoon salt
2   cups nuts, chopped
1   cup (6 ounces) semisweet
     chocolate chips

Preheat the oven to 375 degrees. Beat the butter, shortening, brown sugar, granulated sugar, egg and vanilla in a large mixing bowl until light and fluffy. Stir together the flour, baking powder and salt and add to the sugar mixture, mixing well. Stir in the nuts and chocolate chips. Drop the dough by rounded teaspoonfuls 2 inches apart onto an ungreased cookie sheet. Bake for 8 to 10 minutes or until the edges are lightly browned. Cool on the cookie sheet for 1 minute. Remove the cookies to a wire rack to cool. Wrap in waxed paper and store in a tightly covered container.

Makes 3 to 4 dozen cookies

DOUBLE CHOCOLATE CHIP COOKIES

1/2 cup (1 stick) butter, softened
1/2 cup packed dark brown sugar
1/2 cup granulated sugar
1   egg
1   teaspoon vanilla extract
11/2 cups all-purpose flour
2   tablespoons baking cocoa
1/2 teaspoon baking soda
1/2 teaspoon salt
1   cup (6 ounces) semisweet
     chocolate chips
1/2 cup toffee bits

Preheat the oven to 375 degrees. Beat the butter, brown sugar and granulated sugar in a large mixing bowl until light and fluffy. Beat in the egg and vanilla until smooth. Sift together the flour, baking cocoa, baking soda and salt and add to the butter mixture, mixing well. Stir in the chocolate chips and toffee bits. Drop the dough by rounded teaspoonfuls onto a greased cookie sheet. Bake for 10 minutes or just until firm. Remove the cookies to a wire rack to cool.

Makes 3 to 4 dozen cookies

OAT CRISPS

1   cup (2 sticks) butter, softened
1   cup packed brown sugar
1   cup granulated sugar
1   egg
1   cup vegetable oil
1   teaspoon vanilla extract
1   cup rolled oats
1   cup crushed cornflakes
1   cup shredded coconut (optional)
1/2 cup nuts, chopped
3 1/2 cups all-purpose flour, sifted
1   teaspoon baking soda
1   teaspoon salt

Preheat the oven to 325 degrees. Cream the butter, brown sugar and granulated sugar in a large mixing bowl until light and fluffy. Beat in the egg. Add the oil and vanilla and mix until blended. Stir in the oats, cornflakes, coconut and nuts and mix well. Stir together the flour, baking soda and salt and add to the dough, mixing well. Drop by teaspoonfuls onto an ungreased cookie sheet. Flatten with a fork dipped in water. Bake for 12 minutes. Cool the cookies on the cookie sheet before removing.

Makes 5 to 6 dozen cookies

Susan Culp, President 1982–1983

CRISPY OATMEAL COOKIES

1   cup (2 sticks) unsalted butter, softened
1   cup packed brown sugar
1   cup granulated sugar
2   eggs
1   teaspoon vanilla extract
2   cups unbleached flour
1   teaspoon baking soda
1   teaspoon ground cinnamon
1/2 teaspoon baking powder
1/2 teaspoon salt
1   cup quick-cooking oats
1   cup crisp rice cereal

Preheat the oven to 350 degrees. Cream the butter, brown sugar and granulated sugar in a large mixing bowl until light and fluffy. Beat in the eggs and vanilla. Sift together the flour, baking soda, cinnamon, baking powder and salt. Add to the sugar mixture gradually, beating well after each addition. Fold in the oats and cereal. Drop by tablespoonfuls onto an ungreased cookie sheet. Bake for 9 to 11 minutes or until golden brown. Cool the cookies on the cookie sheet for 1 minute. Remove with a metal spatula to a wire rack to cool.

Makes about 4 dozen cookies

OVERNIGHT COOKIES

2   egg whites, at room temperature
1/4   teaspoon cream of tartar
3/4   cup sugar
      Dash of salt
1/2   teaspoon vanilla extract
1   cup (6 ounces) miniature chocolate-
      coated candy pieces or semisweet
      chocolate chips

Preheat the oven to 375 degrees. Beat the egg whites with the cream of tartar in a deep mixing bowl until stiff peaks form. Add the sugar gradually, beating well after each addition. Add the salt and vanilla. Fold in the candy. Drop by teaspoonfuls onto a greased cookie sheet. Place in the oven and immediately turn off the heat. Leave in the oven for 6 hours to overnight.

Makes 1 1/2 to 2 dozen cookies

Tip: These cookies make a great gift from the kitchen.

SNOWBALLS

1   cup (2 sticks) butter, softened
2   tablespoons granulated sugar
1   egg
2   cups all-purpose flour
1   cup chopped pecans
1   teaspoon vanilla extract
      Confectioners' sugar

Preheat the oven to 350 degrees. Cream the butter, granulated sugar and egg in a large mixing bowl until light and fluffy. Add the flour, pecans and vanilla and mix well. Shape the dough into balls and place on a greased cookie sheet. Bake for 15 to 20 minutes; cool. Roll the cookies in the confectioners' sugar to coat.

Makes about 7 dozen cookies

Paper Bag Apple Crumb Pie

3   or 4 large baking apples, peeled and cut into chunks
1/2   cup sugar
2   tablespoons all-purpose flour
1/2   teaspoon ground nutmeg
1   unbaked (9-inch) pie shell
2   tablespoons lemon juice
1/2   cup sugar
1/2   cup all-purpose flour
1/2   cup (1 stick) cold butter or margarine

Preheat the oven to 425 degrees and position the oven rack in the lowest position. Place the apples in a large bowl. Stir together 1/2 cup sugar, 2 tablespoons flour and the nutmeg and sprinkle over the apples, tossing to coat well. Spoon into the pie shell and drizzle with the lemon juice. Stir together 1/2 cup sugar and 1/2 cup flour in a small bowl. Cut in the butter until crumbly. Sprinkle evenly over the apples. Place the pie in a large heavy nonrecycled brown paper bag. Fold the open end twice and fasten with paper clips. Place on a baking sheet. Bake for 1 hour. Split the bag open and carefully remove the pie; cool.

Serves 6 to 8

Ellen Whitlock, President 1994–1995

Chocolate Brownie Pie

2   tablespoons butter
2   ounces unsweetened chocolate
3/4   cup dark corn syrup
3   eggs
1/2   cup sugar
3/4   cup pecan halves
1   unbaked (9-inch) pie shell
    Whipped cream (optional)

Preheat the oven to 375 degrees. Melt the butter and chocolate with the corn syrup in a heavy saucepan over low heat or in the top of a double boiler. Whisk the eggs and sugar in a large bowl until frothy. Whisk in the chocolate mixture until blended. Stir in the pecans. Pour into the pie shell. Bake for 45 to 50 minutes or just until set; cool. Serve warm or chilled. Garnish with whipped cream or serve with ice cream.

Serves 6 to 8

Ann Mendenhall, President 1951–1952

Tip: *To use baking cocoa instead of the chocolate, sift 1/2 cup baking cocoa with 1/2 cup sugar. Melt 1/4 cup butter in a saucepan with the corn syrup. Whisk the eggs in a large bowl until frothy and whisk in the cocoa mixture until blended. Whisk in the corn syrup mixture. Stir in the pecans. Proceed as directed above.*

Chocolate Peanut Butter Pie

26 foil-wrapped milk chocolate
    kisses, unwrapped
2   tablespoons milk
1   (9-inch) graham cracker pie shell
8   ounces cream cheese, softened
1/2 cup sugar
1   cup peanut butter
8   ounces whipped topping
    Additional foil-wrapped milk chocolate
    kisses, unwrapped

Place the 26 chocolate kisses and the milk
in a microwave-safe bowl. Microwave on
High for 1 minute; stir. Microwave for 30 to
45 seconds longer or until melted; stir until
smooth. Spread evenly over the bottom of
the pie shell. Chill for 30 minutes. Beat the
cream cheese in a medium mixing bowl
until fluffy. Add the sugar gradually, beating
well after each addition. Beat in the peanut
butter. Reserve 1/2 cup of the whipped
topping. Fold the remaining whipped
topping into the peanut butter mixture.
Spoon into the chocolate-lined pie shell.
Chill for 5 hours or until set. Top with the
reserved whipped topping and additional
chocolate kisses.

Serves 6 to 8

Rich Chocolate Pecan Pie

1/2 cup (1 stick) butter, softened
1   cup sugar
1   cup light corn syrup
4   eggs
2   tablespoons bourbon
1   cup (6 ounces) semisweet
    chocolate chips
1   cup pecans, chopped
2   unbaked (9-inch) pie shells

Preheat the oven to 375 degrees. Combine
the butter, sugar and corn syrup in a large
mixing bowl and mix well. Beat in the eggs
and bourbon until smooth. Fold in the
chocolate chips and pecans. Pour into the
pie shells. Bake for 35 to 40 minutes or
until the filling is set.

Serves 12 to 16

Frances B. Armstrong, President 1947–1948

Cocoa Cream Pie

1 1/4 cups sugar
1/2 cup baking cocoa
1/3 cup cornstarch
1/4 teaspoon salt
3 cups milk
3 tablespoons butter
1 1/2 teaspoons vanilla extract
1 (9-inch) baked pie shell or
   crumb pie shell
1 can refrigerated whipped cream, or
   8 ounces whipped topping
   Grated chocolate (optional)

Stir together the sugar, baking cocoa,
cornstarch and salt in a large saucepan.
Add the milk gradually, stirring until
smooth. Cook over medium heat until the
mixture comes to a boil, stirring constantly.
Boil for 1 minute. Remove from the heat
and stir in the butter and vanilla until
blended. Pour into the pie shell. Press a
piece of plastic wrap directly onto the
surface of the pie filling. Chill for 3 to
4 hours. Remove the plastic wrap and
spread the whipped cream over the filling.
Garnish with grated chocolate.

Serves 6 to 8

Coconut Custard Pie

3 eggs
1 cup sugar
1 cup evaporated milk
1 teaspoon vanilla extract
1 unbaked (9-inch) pie shell
1/4 to 1/2 cup flaked coconut

Preheat the oven to 375 degrees. Beat the
eggs in a large mixing bowl until frothy.
Add the sugar, evaporated milk and vanilla
and beat until blended. Pour into the pie
shell and sprinkle with the coconut. Press
the coconut lightly into the filling. Bake for
30 to 40 minutes or until the custard is set.
Chill before slicing.

Serves 8

Grasshopper Pie

CRUST
1 1/2 cups crushed chocolate wafer cookies
1/4   cup butter or margarine, melted

FILLING
32   large marshmallows, or 3 cups miniature marshmallows
1/2   cup milk
1/4   cup crème de menthe
3   tablespoons white crème de cacao
1 1/2 cups chilled heavy cream or whipping cream, whipped
     Several drops of green food coloring
     Shaved semisweet chocolate or chocolate
     wafer crumbs (optional)

For the crust, preheat the oven to 350 degrees. Combine the crushed cookies and the butter in a bowl and mix well. Press on the bottom and up the side of a 9-inch pie plate. Bake for 10 minutes. Cool completely.

For the filling, melt the marshmallows with the milk in a large saucepan over low heat, stirring constantly. Chill until thickened. Stir the marshmallow mixture. Stir in the crème de menthe and the crème de cacao until blended. Fold in the whipped cream. Fold in the food coloring. Pour into the pie crust. Chill for 4 hours or longer. Garnish with shaved chocolate.

Serves 6 to 8

Key Lime Pie

4   egg yolks
1   (14-ounce) can sweetened
      condensed milk
1/2   cup Nellie & Joe's Key West lime juice
      (available at most supermarkets)
1   (9-inch) graham cracker pie shell
      Whipped cream (optional)
      Fresh lime slices (optional)

Preheat the oven to 350 degrees. Whisk the
egg yolks, sweetened condensed milk and
lime juice in a large bowl until smooth and
blended. Pour into the pie shell. Bake for
8 to 10 minutes. Remove from the oven
and cool for 15 minutes or longer. Chill
in the refrigerator for several hours or
overnight. Garnish with whipped cream
and lime slices, if desired.

Serves 6 to 8

Frozen Hawaiian Cream Pie

1   (14-ounce) can fat-free
      sweetened condensed milk
1/3   cup lemon juice
1   (20-ounce) can crushed
      pineapple, drained
2 1/2 to 4 cups shredded coconut
1   cup pecans or walnuts, chopped
8   ounces whipped topping
2   (9-inch) graham cracker pie shells

Combine the sweetened condensed milk,
lemon juice, pineapple, coconut and pecans
in a large bowl and mix well. Fold in the
whipped topping. Pour into the pie shells.
Freeze, covered, for several hours
or overnight.

Serves 12 to 16

Exquisite Pie

1/4 cup (1/2 stick) butter, softened
1 cup sugar
2 eggs
1/2 cup flaked coconut
1/2 cup chopped nuts
1/2 cup raisins
1 tablespoon vinegar
1 teaspoon vanilla extract
1 unbaked (9-inch) pie shell

Preheat the oven to 350 degrees. Beat the butter and sugar in a large mixing bowl until light and fluffy. Beat in the eggs until smooth. Stir in the coconut, nuts, raisins, vinegar and vanilla and mix well. Pour into the pie shell. Bake for 35 minutes or until the filling is set. Let cool.

Serves 6 to 8

Southern Pecan Pie

4 eggs
1/4 cup (1/2 stick) unsalted butter, melted and cooled
1 1/4 cups light corn syrup
1 1/4 cups packed light brown sugar
1 teaspoon vanilla extract
1/2 teaspoon salt
1 unbaked (9- or 10-inch) deep-dish pie shell
1 cup pecans, chopped

Preheat the oven to 350 degrees. Whisk the eggs in a large bowl until frothy. Add the butter, corn syrup, brown sugar, vanilla and salt and mix well. Pour into the pie shell and sprinkle with the pecans. Bake for 45 to 50 minutes; cool.

Serves 6 to 8

Pat Wheeler, President 1990–1991

Tip: To make 3 pies, use 3 regular pie shells (not deep-dish). Double all the filling ingredients except the pecans. Divide the filling among the pie shells and top each with 1 cup pecans. Bake for 30 to 35 minutes or until the filling is set.

Pumpkin Pie

1/2 cup (1 stick) butter, melted
3   cups sugar
3   (15-ounce) cans pumpkin
1   (5-ounce) can evaporated milk
4   eggs
1   teaspoon vanilla extract
1/2 cup sugar
2   heaping tablespoons all-purpose flour
1   teaspoon ground cinnamon
1   teaspoon ground nutmeg
2   unbaked (9- or 10-inch) deep-dish
     pie shells

Preheat the oven to 325 degrees. Combine
the butter and 3 cups sugar in a large
mixing bowl and beat until blended. Add
the pumpkin and evaporated milk and mix
well. Beat in the eggs until blended. Stir in
the vanilla. Stir together 1/2 cup sugar, the
flour, cinnamon and nutmeg and add to the
pumpkin mixture, mixing well. Pour into
the pie shells. Bake for 30 to 35 minutes or
until the filling is set; cool. Serve with
whipped cream, if desired.

Serves 12 to 16

Double-Crust Strawberry Pie

1/2 cup packed brown sugar
2   tablespoons all-purpose flour
1   teaspoon ground cinnamon
1   heaping pint fresh strawberries, hulled
2   frozen pie shells, thawed
2   tablespoons butter, cut into pieces

Preheat the oven to 425 degrees. Stir
together the brown sugar, flour and
cinnamon. Place the strawberries in a large
bowl and sprinkle with the brown sugar
mixture, mixing well. Pour into 1 of the pie
shells. Dot the top with the butter. Remove
the remaining pie shell from the pan and
place over the strawberries. Press the edges
of the pie shells together with a fork to seal.
Cut slits in the top crust. Cover the edge
of the pie with aluminum foil to prevent
overbrowning. Bake for 10 to 15 minutes.
Reduce the oven temperature to 375 degrees
and bake for 15 minutes. Uncover the edge
and bake for 15 minutes longer or until
browned. Cool for 30 minutes before serving.

Serves 6 to 8

Margaret Dalton, President 1953–1954

Sweet Potato Pie

2   eggs
1   cup sugar
1   cup mashed cooked sweet potatoes
1   teaspoon vanilla extract
    Ground cinnamon and nutmeg to taste
1   unbaked (9-inch) pie shell

Preheat the oven to 350 degrees. Beat the eggs and sugar in a large bowl until frothy. Add the sweet potatoes, vanilla, cinnamon and nutmeg and mix well. Pour into the pie shell. Bake for 45 minutes or until the filling is set; cool.

Serves 6 to 8

Easy Pecan Toffee

$1/2$ cup (1 stick) butter
$1/2$ cup (1 stick) margarine
$1/2$ to 1 cup sugar
$1/2$ (16-ounce) package graham crackers, broken into halves
1   cup pecans, chopped

Preheat the oven to 325 degrees. Melt the butter and margarine with the sugar in a saucepan. Bring to a boil; boil for 3 minutes. Place the graham crackers on a rimmed baking sheet. Spoon the hot butter mixture evenly over the crackers. Sprinkle with the pecans. Bake for 10 minutes. Remove to waxed paper and cool completely. Cut or break into pieces.

Makes about 1 pound

Turtle Bars

1   (12-ounce) package vanilla wafers,
    finely crushed
3/4 cup (1 1/2 sticks) butter, melted
1   (10-ounce) package semisweet
    chocolate chips
1   cup pecans, chopped
1   (12-ounce) jar caramel topping

Preheat the oven to 350 degrees. Combine the crushed wafers and butter in a bowl and mix well. Press onto the bottom of a nonstick 9×13-inch baking pan or baking dish. Sprinkle with the chocolate chips and pecans and drizzle with the caramel topping. Bake for 15 to 20 minutes. Cool in the pan on a wire rack. Chill for 45 minutes or longer before cutting into bars. Serve at room temperature. Store in the refrigerator.

Makes 36 to 48 bars

Chocolate- and Pecan-Coated Almond Brittle

3/4 cup (1 1/2 sticks) butter
1 1/4 cups sugar
1 1/2 teaspoons salt
1/4 cup water
1/2 teaspoon baking soda
6   ounces blanched almonds, chopped
     and toasted
12   (1- to 2-ounce) milk chocolate candy
     bars, melted
2   cups chopped pecans

Melt the butter in a large heavy saucepan and add the sugar, salt and water. Bring to a boil over medium-high heat, stirring constantly. Add the baking soda, stirring constantly. The mixture will foam. Cook over medium heat until a candy thermometer registers 320 degrees, stirring frequently. Watch carefully after 280 degrees to prevent scorching. Remove from the heat and stir in the almonds. Pour the mixture onto a large foil-lined buttered baking sheet, spreading evenly. Cool for 5 minutes. Pour half the melted chocolate evenly over the candy. Sprinkle with half the pecans. Chill for 30 minutes. Turn the sheet of candy over and spread with the remaining chocolate. Sprinkle with the remaining pecans. Chill for several hours. Break into pieces. Store tightly covered.

Makes about 2 pounds

CHEESECAKE

CRUST
1¹/2 cups graham cracker crumbs
¹/4 cup sugar
1 teaspoon ground cinnamon
¹/3 cup butter, melted

FILLING
32 ounces cream cheese, softened
4 eggs
1 cup sugar
1 tablespoon lemon juice
  Dash of salt

TOPPING
2 cups sour cream, at room temperature
¹/4 cup sugar
¹/8 teaspoon vanilla extract

For the crust, preheat the oven to 375 degrees. Combine the graham cracker crumbs, sugar, cinnamon and butter in a bowl and mix well. Reserve ¹/2 cup for the topping. Press the remainder onto the bottom of a 10-inch springform pan.

For the filling, beat the cream cheese in a large mixing bowl until light and fluffy. Beat the eggs and sugar in a medium bowl until thick and smooth. Add to the cream cheese. Add the lemon juice and salt and mix well. Pour into the crust. Bake for 30 minutes or until the center is nearly set. Remove from the oven. Increase the oven temperature to 475 degrees.

For the topping, combine the sour cream, sugar and vanilla in a small bowl and mix well. Spread over the cheesecake. Sprinkle with the reserved crumbs. Return to the oven and bake for 10 minutes. Cool on a wire rack. Chill in the pan for several hours or overnight. Let stand at room temperature for 1 hour before serving. Place on a serving platter and remove the side of the pan.

Serves 12 to 16

Susan Samuel, President 1987–1988

Cheesecake with Pineapple Glaze

CRUST

1³/4	cups graham cracker crumbs
1/3	cup butter, softened
1/4	cup sugar

FILLING

40	ounces cream cheese, softened
1³/4	cups sugar
3	tablespoons all-purpose flour
5	eggs
2	egg yolks
1	tablespoon grated lemon zest
1/4	cup heavy cream or whipping cream

GLAZE

2	tablespoons sugar
4	teaspoons cornstarch
2	(8-ounce) cans syrup-pack crushed pineapple
2	tablespoons lemon juice
2	drops of yellow food coloring (optional)

For the crust, preheat the oven to 475 degrees. Remove the side of a 10-inch springform pan. Place a piece of waxed paper over the bottom of the pan and fasten the side in place. Cut off the excess waxed paper on the outside of the pan. Butter the side and waxed paper-lined bottom of the pan. Combine the graham cracker crumbs, butter and sugar in a bowl and mix well. Press firmly onto the bottom and up the side of the prepared pan.

For the filling, beat the cream cheese in a large mixing bowl until light and fluffy. Add the sugar gradually, beating well after each addition. Sprinkle with the flour and mix well. Beat in the eggs and egg yolks 1 at a time. Add the lemon zest and cream and beat at low speed until combined. Pour into the crust. Bake for 12 minutes. Reduce the oven temperature to 250 degrees and bake for 1¹/2 hours. Turn off the oven and leave the cheesecake in the oven for 30 minutes with the door ajar. Remove to a wire rack to cool completely. Chill in the pan for several hours or overnight. Place on a serving platter and remove the side of the pan.

For the glaze, stir together the sugar and cornstarch in a saucepan. Stir in the undrained pineapple until combined. Stir in the lemon juice and food coloring. Cook over low heat until thickened, stirring constantly; cool. Spread over the top of the cheesecake.

Serves 12 to 16

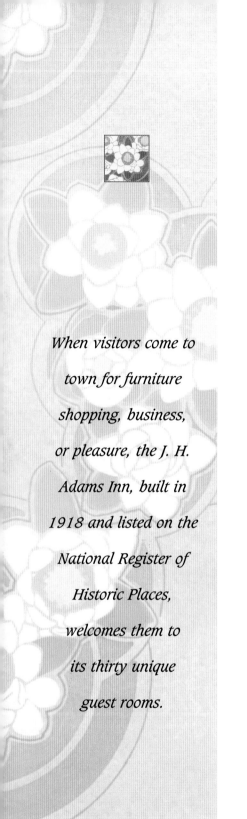

PEACH COBBLER

4	cups sliced peeled peaches
1/2	cup packed brown sugar
1/2	cup granulated sugar
	Dash of ground nutmeg
1	cup all-purpose flour
1	cup granulated sugar
1	teaspoon baking powder
1/4	teaspoon salt
1	egg, beaten
1	teaspoon vanilla extract
6	tablespoons butter, melted
1/4	cup granulated sugar

Preheat the oven to 350 degrees. Combine the peaches, brown sugar, 1/2 cup granulated sugar and nutmeg in a large bowl and mix well. Pour into a 2-quart baking dish. Stir together the flour, 1 cup granulated sugar, the baking powder and salt in a medium bowl. Add the egg and vanilla, mixing with a fork until crumbly. Sprinkle the topping over the peaches and drizzle with the butter. Sprinkle with 1/4 cup granulated sugar. Bake for 40 minutes or until the top is browned.

Serves 8

Banana Fritters with Lemon Sauce

FRITTERS

1	cup all-purpose flour
2	teaspoons baking powder
2	tablespoons confectioners' sugar
	Pinch of salt
1	egg, beaten
1/4	cup (or more) milk
2	tablespoons butter, melted
3	bananas, mashed
	Vegetable oil for deep-frying
	Additional confectioners' sugar (optional)

LEMON SAUCE

1/2	cup sugar
1	tablespoon cornstarch
1/8	teaspoon salt
1/8	teaspoon ground nutmeg
1	cup boiling water
2	tablespoons butter
1/2	tablespoon lemon juice

For the fritters, stir together the flour, baking powder, 2 tablespoons confectioners' sugar and salt in a large mixing bowl and make a well in the center. Add the egg, milk and melted butter and stir just until blended. Stir in the bananas just until combined, adding additional milk if the batter is too thick. Heat vegetable oil to 375 degrees in a large heavy pan. Drop the batter by tablespoonfuls into the hot oil a few at a time and cook until golden brown on both sides. The fritters should turn themselves over; if not, turn them when the first side has browned. Remove with a slotted spoon to paper towels. Cool slightly and sprinkle with confectioners' sugar, if desired.

For the sauce, stir together the sugar, cornstarch, salt and nutmeg in a small saucepan. Add the water gradually, stirring until smooth. Cook over medium heat until thickened and clear, stirring frequently. Stir in the butter and lemon juice and mix well. Pour over the warm fritters or use as a dipping sauce.

Serves 4 to 6

Helen Millis, President 1932–1934

Milky Way Ice Cream

12 (16-ounce) Milky Way candy bars,
    cut into chunks
1   (14-ounce) can sweetened
    condensed milk
1   (5-ounce) can chocolate syrup
8   cups milk

Microwave the candy bars and the
sweetened condensed milk in a large
microwave-safe bowl on High for 2 minutes
or until the candy is melted, stirring after
each minute. Beat with an electric mixer
until smooth. Add the chocolate syrup and
mix well. Beat in the milk gradually until
blended. Pour into an ice cream freezer
container and freeze according to the
manufacturer's directions.

Serves 8

Lemon Sponge Cups

3   eggs
1   cup granulated sugar
2   tablespoons all-purpose flour
     Grated zest of 2 lemons (optional)
1/4 cup lemon juice
1   cup milk
     Confectioners' sugar (optional)
     Mint leaves and fresh berries
     (optional)

Preheat the oven to 325 degrees. Beat
the eggs, granulated sugar and flour in a
large mixing bowl until smooth and thick.
Stir in the lemon zest and lemon juice. Add
the milk and mix well. Strain the mixture
and pour into 4 buttered 3/4-cup ramekins
or custard cups. Place the ramekins in a
roasting pan or other deep baking pan and
pour hot water in the pan until halfway
up the sides of the cups. Bake for 50 to
60 minutes or until the tops of the custards
are firm. Remove the ramekins from the
water bath and cool. Chill for several hours
or overnight. To serve, sprinkle with
confectioners' sugar and garnish with
mint leaves and berries, if desired.

Serves 4

*Tip: Recipe can be doubled. These sponge
cups are a great make-ahead dessert for a
dinner party.*

Almond Cream Puff Ring

PUFF RING

1   cup water
1/2 cup (1 stick) butter
1/4 teaspoon salt
1   cup all-purpose flour
4   eggs
1   (4-ounce) package vanilla instant
     pudding mix
11/4 cups milk
1   cup heavy cream or whipping cream,
     whipped
1   teaspoon almond extract

CHOCOLATE GLAZE

1/2 cup (3 ounces) semisweet
     chocolate chips
1   tablespoon butter
11/2 teaspoons milk
11/2 teaspoons light corn syrup

For the puff ring, preheat the oven to 400 degrees. Combine the water, butter, and salt in a saucepan and bring to a boil over medium heat. Remove from the heat. Add the flour stirring vigorously with a wooden spoon until the mixture forms a ball and pulls away from the side of the pan. Beat in the eggs 1 at a time, beating until the mixture is smooth and satiny; cool slightly. Lightly grease and flour a large baking sheet. Trace a 7-inch circle in the flour. Drop the batter by heaping tablespoonfuls into 10 mounds inside the circle to form a ring. Bake for 40 minutes or until golden brown. Turn off the oven and leave the ring in the oven for 15 minutes. Remove to a wire rack to cool completely. Prepare the pudding mix with 11/4 cups milk, using the package directions. Fold in the whipped cream and almond extract. Slice the puff ring horizontally in half and place the puff ring on a serving platter. Spoon the filling into the bottom of the puff ring and replace the top; chill.

For the glaze, heat all the ingredients in the top of a double boiler over hot but not boiling water or in a heavy 1-quart saucepan over low heat, stirring until smooth. Drizzle over the puff ring.

Serves 10

Kay Snow, President 1988–1989

Make-Ahead Banana Split Supreme

CRUST

1   (12-ounce) package vanilla wafers, crushed

3/4 cup (1 1/2 sticks) margarine, melted

FILLING

2   egg whites

2   cups confectioners' sugar

1   cup (2 sticks) margarine, melted

4   large bananas

1   (20-ounce) can crushed pineapple, drained

8   ounces whipped topping

3/4 cup nuts, chopped

1   (4-ounce) jar maraschino cherries, drained and quartered

For the crust, combine the crushed wafers and the margarine in a bowl and mix well. Press onto the bottom and up the sides of a 9×13-inch dish.

For the filling, beat the egg whites, confectioners' sugar and margarine until smooth and blended. Pour into the crust. Slice the bananas evenly over the top. Spoon the pineapple over the bananas. Spread the whipped topping evenly over the pineapple and sprinkle with the nuts. Top with the cherries. Chill, covered, for 24 hours before serving.

Serves 12 to 16

Molten Chocolate Cakes with Chocolate Mint Sauce

CAKES

5   ounces bittersweet or semisweet chocolate

10   tablespoons (1 stick plus 2 tablespoons) unsalted butter

3   eggs

3   egg yolks

1$1/2$ cups confectioners' sugar

$1/2$ cup all-purpose flour

CHOCOLATE MINT SAUCE

4$1/2$ ounces bittersweet or semisweet chocolate

2   ounces unsweetened chocolate

$1/3$ cup hot water

$1/4$ cup light corn syrup

$3/4$ teaspoon peppermint extract

For the cakes, preheat the oven to 450 degrees. Melt the chocolate and butter in the top of a double boiler over hot but not boiling water or in a heavy saucepan over low heat, stirring until smooth; cool slightly. Whisk the eggs and egg yolks in a large bowl until well blended. Whisk in the confectioners' sugar, melted chocolate and flour until smooth. Pour into 6 buttered individual ramekins or a soufflé dish. Place on a baking sheet. Bake for 11 minutes or until the sides are set but the centers are still soft.

For the sauce, melt the chocolate in the top of a double boiler over hot but not boiling water or in a small heavy saucepan over low heat, stirring until smooth; cool slightly. Whisk together the water, corn syrup and peppermint extract in a small bowl. Whisk into the melted chocolate until smooth.

To serve, run a knife around the edge of each ramekin to loosen the cake. Place a serving plate over each ramekin and invert the cake onto the plate. Serve warm with warm Chocolate Mint Sauce.

Serves 6

Tip: The cakes and sauce can be prepared ahead. Prepare the cake batter and pour into the ramekins as above. Refrigerate the unbaked ramekins for up to 1 day. Bake for 14 minutes. Proceed as directed above. Prepare the sauce as directed above and refrigerate for up to 2 days. Reheat the sauce before serving.

DEATH BY CHOCOLATE

1   (21-ounce) package brownie mix
1/4 cup coffee mixed with
     1 teaspoon sugar
2   (4-ounce) packages chocolate instant
     pudding mix
1   (10-ounce) package milk chocolate-
     covered toffee bits, crushed
12 ounces whipped topping

Prepare and bake the brownie mix using the package directions for a 9×13-inch baking pan. Cool completely. Poke holes in the top of the brownie layer using a fork and drizzle with the coffee. Prepare the pudding mix using the package directions. Break up the brownie into small pieces and place half the pieces in a large glass serving bowl or trifle dish. Top the brownie pieces with 1/2 of the pudding, 1/3 of the crushed toffee and 1/2 of the whipped topping. Repeat the layers using the remaining brownie pieces, remaining pudding, 1/2 of the remaining toffee and the remaining whipped topping. Sprinkle with the remaining toffee. Chill, covered, for 2 hours or longer before serving.

Serves 12 to 16

BANANA PUDDING

3   egg yolks
1 1/4 cups sugar
1/2 cup all-purpose flour
3   cups milk
1/2 teaspoon vanilla extract
1   (12-ounce) package vanilla wafers
4   or 5 bananas, sliced

Whisk the egg yolks in a large saucepan until thick and smooth. Whisk in the sugar and flour until blended. Add the milk and whisk until blended. Bring to a boil over medium heat, stirring constantly. Cook until slightly thickened, stirring constantly. Remove from the heat and stir in the vanilla. Cool slightly. Place a layer of vanilla wafers in the bottom of a 9×13-inch dish. Top with a layer of sliced bananas, then a layer of the pudding. Continue layering the wafers, bananas and pudding until the dish is full, ending with a layer of wafers; chill. Garnish each serving with a dollop of whipped cream, if desired.

Serves 8

Butterscotch Pecan Torte with Butterscotch Sauce

TORTE

6	egg yolks
1¹/2	cups sugar
1	teaspoon baking powder
2	teaspoons vanilla extract
1	teaspoon almond extract
6	egg whites, at room temperature
2	cups graham cracker crumbs
1	cup pecans, chopped

BUTTERSCOTCH SAUCE

2	eggs
1	cup packed brown sugar
¹/4	cup (¹/2 stick) butter
1¹/4	cups orange juice
¹/4	cup water
¹/2	teaspoon vanilla extract
	Whipped cream (optional)
	Chopped nuts (optional)

For the torte, preheat the oven to 325 degrees. Beat the egg yolks in a large mixing bowl until thick and smooth. Stir together the sugar and baking powder and add to the egg yolks gradually, beating well after each addition. Stir in the vanilla and almond extract. Beat the egg whites in a deep mixing bowl until stiff glossy peaks form. Fold the egg whites into the batter gradually. Fold in the graham cracker crumbs and pecans. Pour into a 9-inch springform pan. Bake for 50 to 55 minutes. Cool in the pan on a wire rack.

For the sauce, beat the eggs in a large saucepan until frothy. Add the brown sugar, butter, orange juice and water. Bring to a boil over medium heat, stirring constantly. Reduce the heat and cook until thickened, stirring constantly. Stir in the vanilla; chill.

To serve, place the torte on a serving platter and remove the side of the pan. Spoon the Butterscotch Sauce over the torte. Garnish with dollops of whipped cream and a sprinkling of nuts, if desired.

Serves 12 to 14

ENGLISH TRIFLE

2 cups heavy cream or whipping cream
4 egg yolks
1/2 cup packed brown sugar
1 tablespoon all-purpose flour
1/8 teaspoon salt
1/4 teaspoon vanilla extract
1/8 teaspoon almond extract
1/4 cup golden sherry
10 stale ladyfingers, split
1/3 cup raspberry jam
1/2 cup blanched slivered almonds

Heat the cream in the top of a double boiler or in a saucepan placed over boiling water. Beat the egg yolks in a medium bowl until thick and smooth. Add the brown sugar, flour and salt and mix well. Add the hot cream slowly, stirring constantly. Return the mixture to the top of the double boiler and cook until thickened, stirring constantly. The custard should coat a metal spoon. Stir in the vanilla and almond extract. Press a piece of plastic wrap directly on the surface of the custard and chill. Sprinkle the sherry over the ladyfingers and arrange on the bottom and side of a 1-quart trifle dish or glass serving bowl. Spread the jam over the bottom ladyfingers. Reserve 2 tablespoons of the almonds. Sprinkle the remaining almonds over the jam layer. Pour the chilled custard over the almonds. Sprinkle with the reserved almonds. Chill, covered, for 12 hours.

Serves 6 to 8

Lillian Leath, President 1959–1960

RASPBERRY-CHAMPAGNE SORBET

3/4   cup sugar
3/4   cup water
1   pint fresh raspberries
1/4   cup water
2   cups chilled Champagne

Combine the sugar and 3/4 cup water in a small saucepan and bring to a boil. Cook until the sugar dissolves, stirring constantly. Remove from the heat and cool completely. Purée the raspberries and 1/4 cup water in a food processor or blender. Strain and discard the seeds. Combine the sugar syrup, raspberry purée and Champagne in a bowl and mix well. Pour into an ice cream freezer container and freeze using the manufacturer's directions. Spoon into a freezer-proof container and freeze for at least 1 hour.

Serves 6 to 8

THICK FUDGE SAUCE

3   ounces unsweetened chocolate
2   cups confectioners' sugar, sifted
2/3   cup evaporated milk
3   tablespoons butter
1/8   teaspoon salt
1/2   teaspoon vanilla extract

Melt the chocolate in a medium saucepan over low heat. Add the confectioners' sugar gradually, beating well after each addition. Stir in the evaporated milk and cook until thickened, stirring constantly. Add the butter and salt and stir until the butter is melted. Remove from the heat and stir in the vanilla. Serve warm. Store in the refrigerator. Reheat to serve. If the sauce is too thick, add a small amount of cream or evaporated milk when reheating.

Makes about 3 cups

FROM OUR
LOCAL
CHEFS

Southern Roots' Angel Biscuits Stuffed with Pimento Cheese

ANGEL BISCUITS

2	envelopes dry yeast
1/2	cup warm water
5	cups all-purpose flour
2	tablespoons sugar
2	tablespoons baking powder
3/4	teaspoon baking soda
3/4	teaspoon salt
1	cup vegetable shortening
1	to 11/2 cups buttermilk
	Melted butter

SMOKED GOUDA, WHITE CHEDDAR AND PARMESAN PIMENTO CHEESE

1	cup (4 ounces) shredded smoked Gouda cheese
1	cup (4 ounces) shredded white Cheddar cheese
1	cup (4 ounces) grated Parmesan cheese
1	roasted red pepper, finely chopped
1/2	to 3/4 cup mayonnaise
1	tablespoon honey

For the biscuits, preheat the oven to 400 degrees. Dissolve the yeast in the water in a small bowl. Sift the flour, sugar, baking powder, baking soda and salt together into a bowl. Cut in the shortening. Add the buttermilk and yeast mixture and knead until smooth. Roll out on a floured surface. Cut with a 1-inch biscuit cutter. Arrange on a baking sheet. Bake for 13 to 15 minutes or until light brown on top. Brush with melted butter.

For the pimento cheese, combine the cheese, red pepper, mayonnaise and honey in a bowl and mix well, adding additional mayonnaise if necessary to reach the desired consistency. Serve on the Angel Biscuits.

Serves about 30

M. Stephen's Rock Shrimp Spring Roll with Ginger-Blue Cheese Dipping Sauce

GINGER-BLUE CHEESE DIPPING SAUCE

1/2   cup crumbled blue cheese
1   tablespoon finely chopped ginger
1   teaspoon minced fresh garlic
1   teaspoon finely chopped shallot
      Juice of 2 lemons
      Juice of 1 orange
2   tablespoons sour cream
2   tablespoons soy sauce
1   tablespoon maple syrup

ROCK SHRIMP SPRING ROLL

12   rock shrimp, chopped
1   teaspoon minced fresh garlic
      Salt and pepper to taste
8   pieces rice paper
2   tablespoons finely chopped
      English cucumber
2   tablespoons red pepper

For the sauce, combine the cheese, ginger, garlic, shallot, lemon juice, orange juice, sour cream, soy sauce and maple syrup in a bowl and mix well.

For the spring roll, sauté the shrimp, garlic, salt and pepper in a skillet over medium heat until the shrimp turn pink and begin to curl. Combine the shrimp and a small amount of the sauce in a bowl and toss gently to coat. Run cold water over 2 pieces of rice paper for 1 minute. Place 1/4 of the shrimp on the rice paper. Sprinkle with 1/4 of the cucumber and red pepper. Roll the rice paper to enclose the filling. Repeat the procedure with the remaining ingredients. Serve on a platter with fresh herbs and the remaining dipping sauce.

Serves 4

Aquaria Seafood Grill's Crab Cakes

1 pound lump crab meat
1 egg, beaten
1 teaspoon Dijon mustard
1 teaspoon chopped fresh parsley
1 teaspoon Old Bay Seasoning
1 teaspoon Texas Pete hot sauce
1 teaspoon Worcestershire sauce
1 teaspoon lemon juice
1/4 cup mayonnaise
1/4 cup chopped red bell pepper
1/4 cup chopped green onions

Combine the crab meat, egg, Dijon mustard, parsley, Old Bay seasoning, hot sauce, Worcestershire sauce, lemon juice, mayonnaise, bell pepper and green onions in a bowl and mix well. Shape into patties. Cook in a nonstick skillet over medium heat for 2 to 3 minutes per side or until golden brown.

Serves 8

Real Creations' Goat Cheese Log with Sun-Dried Tomatoes and Rosemary

1/4 cup chopped sun-dried tomatoes with herbs in olive oil
1 garlic clove, minced
1 tablespoon minced fresh rosemary
1 teaspoon extra-virgin olive oil
1 (8-ounce) log goat cheese
    Fresh rosemary sprigs

Combine the sun-dried tomatoes, garlic, rosemary and olive oil in a bowl and mix well. Place the goat cheese log on a medium serving platter. Spoon the tomato mixture over the goat cheese. Garnish with rosemary sprigs. Serve with crackers.

Serves 8

Big Ed's Chicken Pit's Barbecue Slaw

3/4   cup sugar
11/2 cups ketchup
1   cup cider vinegar
11/2 tablespoons hot red pepper sauce
1   tablespoon salt
1   tablespoon pepper
3   to 4 heads cabbage, shredded
1/2   cup finely chopped dill pickles

Combine the sugar, ketchup, vinegar, hot sauce, salt and pepper in a large bowl and stir until the sugar is dissolved. Add the cabbage and pickles and mix well. Store, tightly covered, in the refrigerator for up to 3 weeks.

Makes about 1 gallon

String and Splinter Club's Summer Tomato Pie

1   unbaked (9-inch) deep-dish pie shell
2   to 3 large tomatoes, peeled and thickly sliced
1   large red onion, chopped
      Fresh basil, chopped
      Salt and pepper to taste
1   cup mayonnaise
1   cup (4 ounces) shredded sharp Cheddar cheese

Preheat the oven to 350 degrees. Prick the pie shell 4 or 5 times with a fork. Bake for 4 to 6 minutes or until golden brown. Set aside to cool. Layer the tomatoes and onion alternately in the cooled pie shell, sprinkling each layer with basil, salt and pepper. Combine the mayonnaise and cheese in a bowl and mix well. Spread over the top layer. Bake for 20 minutes or until bubbly. Serve immediately.

Serves 6 to 8

Tip: *To minimize the amount of liquid in the tomatoes and keep the pie from being too runny, you may sprinkle the sliced tomatoes lightly with salt and let drain on a cooling rack for 20 minutes prior to placing in the pie shell.*

Parson's Table Croutons

2   to 3 sticks (1 to 1 1/2 cups)
     butter, melted
2   to 3 tablespoons Worcestershire sauce
1   tablespoon garlic powder or
     onion powder
1   gallon bread cubes
1 1/2 ounces Parmesan cheese, grated

Preheat the oven to 250 degrees. Combine
the butter, Worcestershire sauce and garlic
powder in a bowl and mix well. Arrange
2 layers of the bread cubes in a large
roasting pan. Pour about 1/3 of the butter
mixture over the bread and toss to coat.
Sprinkle with 1/3 of the cheese. Bake for
1 1/2 hours, stirring every 15 minutes.
Watch carefully to avoid burning the bread.
Repeat the process with the remaining
ingredients until all of the bread cubes
have been baked.

Makes 1 gallon croutons

Emerywood Fine Foods' House Chicken Salad

1   pound roasted chicken breast, cubed
1/4 cup mayonnaise, or more to taste
1/2 cup finely chopped mixed red and
     green bell peppers
1   tablespoon finely chopped
     fresh rosemary
     Salt and pepper to taste
     Mixed greens

Combine the chicken, mayonnaise, bell
peppers and rosemary in a bowl and mix
well. Season with salt and pepper. Chill,
covered, until ready to serve. Serve over
mixed greens or on your favorite bread.

Serves 4

Giannos' Marinara Sauce

1	cup extra-virgin olive oil
4	cups finely chopped onions
1/2	cup chopped fresh garlic
1/4	cup chopped fresh parsley
1/4	cup chopped fresh basil
12	cups finely chopped canned tomatoes
1	tablespoon sugar
1	tablespoon chopped fresh oregano

Heat the olive oil in a large saucepan. Add the onions and garlic and sauté until tender. Add the parsley, basil and tomatoes and cook over medium-low heat for 1 1/2 hours, stirring occasionally. Stir in the sugar and oregano. Serve with your favorite pasta.

Serves 15 to 20

Pomodoro's Bourbon Brown Sugar-Mustard Glaze for Salmon

1/4	cup bourbon
1/2	cup packed dark brown sugar
1	teaspoon Champagne vinegar
1	cup grainy mustard
1/2	cup Dijon mustard

Heat the bourbon in a saucepan until the alcohol has burned off. Combine the brown sugar and vinegar in a bowl and mix well. Add the bourbon, grainy mustard and Dijon mustard and mix well. Brush the glaze over salmon and cook using your desired method.

Makes 2 1/4 cups, or enough for 8 pieces of salmon

Blue Water Grille's Barbecue Duck Confit with Collard Greens

DUCK

1/4	cup kosher salt
2	tablespoons pepper
1	tablespoon dried basil
1	tablespoon dried thyme
4	duck hindquarters
2	pounds rendered duck fat
1	orange, sliced
3	bay leaves

COLLARD GREENS

5	slices smoked bacon
1	tablespoon chopped bacon
3	tablespoons olive oil
2	garlic cloves, chopped
1	bunch collard greens
1/2	gallon chicken stock
3/4	cup red wine vinegar
3/4	cup white vinegar
1	tablespoon hot red pepper sauce
1 1/2	tablespoons kosher salt
1/2	tablespoon pepper

For the duck, combine the salt, pepper, basil and thyme in a bowl and mix well. Rub the mixture over the duck. Chill, covered, for 8 to 10 hours. Preheat the oven to 225 degrees. Place the duck in a baking dish and cover with the duck fat. Arrange the orange slices and bay leaves around the duck. Bake for 4 1/2 hours.

For the collard greens, cook the bacon in the olive oil in a large saucepan over low heat until the fat melts. Add the garlic and collard greens and cook for 1 minute over medium heat, stirring constantly. Add the chicken stock, red wine vinegar, white vinegar, hot sauce, salt and pepper and mix well. Bring to a boil and boil for 10 minutes, stirring frequently. Simmer over medium heat for 45 minutes. Adjust the seasonings.

BARBECUE SAUCE

1 1/2   cups water

1 1/2   cups ketchup

1/2   cup Worcestershire sauce

3/4   cup cider vinegar

1/2   cup packed light brown sugar

2   tablespoons dry mustard

2   tablespoons chili powder

For the barbecue sauce, combine the water, ketchup, Worcestershire sauce, vinegar, brown sugar, dry mustard and chili powder in a saucepan over medium heat. Simmer for 15 minutes, stirring occasionally.

To assemble, divide the collard greens among 4 dinner plates. Place the duck on the collard greens and ladle the barbecue sauce over the top.

Serves 4

Tip: *You may substitute 1/2 gallon of water and 2 chicken bouillon cubes for the chicken stock used in preparation of the collard greens, if desired.*

High Point Country Club's Ice Cream Pie

1   egg white, beaten
1   graham cracker pie shell
       Vanilla ice cream, softened
1/4   cup egg meringue powder
1   (8-ounce) jar marshmallow creme
       Thick Fudge Sauce (page 187), or
       1 jar of favorite hot fudge sauce
       Whipped cream
       Strawberry halves

Preheat the oven to 350 degrees. Brush the egg white over the pie shell. Bake for 5 minutes or until the crust is dry. Remove from the oven and let stand until cool. Spoon ice cream into the pie shell. Store in the freezer until the ice cream is frozen. Prepare the meringue powder using the package directions and mix until stiff peaks form. Add the marshmallow creme and mix well. Spoon over the ice cream. Brown with a butane torch or place in a preheated oven and broil for a few seconds, watching closely so that the ice cream does not melt. Freeze until ready to serve. To serve, heat the fudge sauce. Cut the pie into portions and ladle the fudge sauce over each portion. Garnish each serving with a dollop of whipped cream and a strawberry half.

Serves 6 to 8

J. Basul Noble's Currant Raisin and Cognac Bread Pudding

BREAD PUDDING

1	cup currant raisins
1/2	cup good-quality Cognac
2/3	stick butter, melted
1	baguette, or 1/2 loaf white bread or brioche, cubed
4	eggs
1 1/2	cups milk
1 1/2	cups heavy cream or whipping cream
2/3	cup sugar
1	teaspoon salt

CARAMEL SAUCE

1/2	cup sugar
1/4	cup water
	Heavy cream or whipping cream to taste
	Butter to taste

For the bread pudding, combine the raisins and Cognac in a small bowl and let stand for 1 to 2 hours. Combine the butter and bread cubes in a bowl and toss gently to coat. Let stand to allow the butter to soak in. Combine the eggs, milk, cream, sugar and salt in a large bowl and mix well. Add the bread cubes and toss gently to coat. Add the raisin mixture. Let stand for 2 hours. Preheat the oven to 350 degrees. Spoon the bread mixture into a buttered and sugared baking mold. Bake for 45 to 60 minutes or until the center is set.

For the sauce, cook the sugar in a saucepan over low heat until it begins to caramelize, stirring frequently. Remove from the heat and add the water gradually, stirring constantly. Whisk in the cream and butter. Serve over the bread pudding.

Serves 6 to 8

Tip: If you would prefer to bake the pudding in individual baking molds, preheat the oven to 450 degrees and bake for 20 to 25 minutes or until the centers are set.

CONTRIBUTORS AND TESTERS

*We would like to thank all of our friends, family, and members of the
Junior League of High Point for the countless hours they generously devoted to collecting
and testing recipes. Their tireless efforts are reflected in the pages of this cookbook.
We express our deepest gratitude to those listed below and apologize to anyone we
may have inadvertently failed to mention.*

Caryl Adams
Martha Mitchell Adams
Mary Ragsdale Adkins
Chris Amos
Madeline Amos
Martha Amos
Peggy Amos
Roma Amos
Nancy Anderson
Anne Andrews
Aquaria Seafood Grill
Cindy Armfield
Frances B. Armstrong
Cathy Arthur
Shea Barnett
Lynn Bass
Laura B. Beck
Sara Bencini
Courtney Best
Pattie Betts
Kendra Biddle
Big Ed's Chicken Pit
Donna Blakely
Emily Bland
Susie Bland
Wanna Blanton
Blue Water Grille

Alisha Boger
Kitty Boone
Edith Brady
Teresa Bretzmann
Ann Busby
Amy Bland Carroll
Libby Cheek
Lyl Clinard
MacLean Clinard
Jill Clodfelter
Kitty Coble
Debbie Cottam
Evie Cottam
Wink Cottam
Barbara Coughlin
Helen Covington
Katherine Covington
Kristen Craver
Penny Cridlebaugh
Ashley Culler
Esther Culp
Susan Culp
Teenie Dallas
Vicki Dallas
Margaret Dalton
Beth Dasher
Doris Dowdy

Tricia Doyle
Beth Earnst
Shay Edwards
Emerywood Fine Foods
Melanie Eskew
Lore Fariss
Gidget Fletcher
Allison Forrester
Sarah Foscue
Courtney Freedle
Ann Freeze
Mazie Froelich
Lane Fulton
Sandra Funk
Connie Gaines
Lorraine Gayle
Barbara Perry Geddie
Irma Geddie
Giannos Stone Oven Pizzaria
Marybeth Grein
Chris Grimes
Malia Grimes
Luci Gulledge
Colleen Hales
Carol Hall
Tammy Hamilton
Mary Wray Hamrick

Margaret Hart
Chris Hayes
Jennie Jarrell Hayman
Pat Heery
Kim Heiman
Virginia Hicks
High Point Country Club
Betsy Hoak
Karen Hoffman
Peggy Honeycutt
Bonnie Horney
Betty Ann Hubbard
Judy Hustrulid
Betsy Hutchens
Cindy Jarrell
Mary Jarrell
Zola Jones
Mary Lib C. Joyce
Louise Kearns
Susan Keaton
Katharine W. Kelly
Nan Kester
Joy Key
Nancy Laney
Abbie Lassiter
Aimee Lassiter
Joan Lawrence
Lillian Leath
Penny Leonard
Barbara Levina
Margaret Lewis
Sue Lewis
Nancy Lyles
Ann Lynch
Mary Geddie Lyon
Lee Ann Magnusson
Lois Markham

Eva Dell Marsh
Odelle Marsh
Pearl Marsh
Betty Martin
Harriet Mattes
Cornelia McCuiston
Ann Mendenhall
Judy Mendenhall
Avery Merritt
Helen Millis
Kitty Montgomery
Laney Morris
Susan Morris
Monnie Murray
J. Basul Noble's
Donna Nottoli
Christy Oliver
Parson's Table
Celeste Coker Payne
Kandace Perryman
Kay Phillips
Pomodoro Restaurant
    and Catering
Irma Price
Real Creations
Phebe Roberson
Liz Rogers
Allison Russell
Susan Samuel
Joy Craven Scott
Elizabeth Sheffield
Regina Shillinglaw
Meredith Slane
Debbie Smothers
Kay Snow
Virginia McNeil Snow
Southern Roots

Judith Stalder
Kelly Steadman
M. Stephen's
Mary Louise Stone
Jupy Stout
String and Splinter Club
Laurie Tester
Beth Thomas
Fran Thomas
Bootsy Tucker
Nell Tucker
Britt Armfield Tyson
Judy Culp Walker
Elizabeth "Bonie" Wall
Lucie Wall
Joan Walser
Julie Walters
Nancy Warburton
Lou Washburn
Linda Wheeler
Pat Wheeler
Gena White
Ellen Whitlock
Meryle Wilson
Nicole Wilson
Karen Wint
Evelyn Wood
Nathalie Wood
Sarah Woollen
Lee Worden
Becky Wyatt
Meredith Yow
Maryann Zutaut

INDEX

Furniture City Feasts, Restored

A Collection of Recipes from the Junior League of High Point

707 Westchester Drive, Suite 103

High Point, North Carolina 27262

Telephone 336-889-5479 • Fax 336-889-8508

Name

Street Address

City   State   Zip

Telephone

YOUR ORDER	QUANTITY	TOTAL
Furniture City Feasts, Restored at $29.95 per book		$
Postage and handling at $7.50 per book		$
TOTAL		$

Method of Payment: [   ] MasterCard   [   ] VISA
                       [   ] Check payable to Junior League of High Point, Inc.

Account Number   Expiration Date

Signature

Photocopies will be accepted.